Just *one* Charm Pack QUILTS

Cheryl Brickey

BUST Your Precut Stash
with 18 Projects in 2 Colorways

stash BOOKS
an imprint of C&T Publishing

PUBLISHER: Amy Barrett-Daffin

CREATIVE DIRECTOR: Gailen Runge

ACQUISITIONS EDITOR: Roxane Cerda

MANAGING EDITOR: Liz Aneloski

EDITOR: Beth Baumgartel

TECHNICAL EDITOR: Gailen Runge

COVER/BOOK DESIGNER: April Mostek

PRODUCTION COORDINATOR: Tim Manibusan

PRODUCTION EDITOR: Alice Mace Nakanishi

ILLUSTRATOR: Cheryl Brickey

PHOTO ASSISTANTS: Lauren Herberg and Gabriel Martinez

PHOTOGRAPHY by Estefany Gonzalez of C&T Publishing, Inc., unless otherwise noted

Published by Stash Books, an imprint of C&T Publishing, Inc., P.O. Box 1456, Lafayette, CA 94549

Attention Copy Shops: Please note the following exception—publisher and author give permission to photocopy pages 123–127 for personal use only.

Attention Teachers: C&T Publishing, Inc., encourages the use of our books as texts for teaching. You can find lesson plans for many of our titles at ctpub.com or contact us at ctinfo@ctpub.com or 800-284-1114.

We take great care to ensure that the information included in our products is accurate and presented in good faith, but no warranty is provided, nor are results guaranteed. Having no control over the choices of materials or procedures used, neither the author nor C&T Publishing, Inc., shall have any liability to any person or entity with respect to any loss or damage caused directly or indirectly by the information contained in this book. For your convenience, we post an up-to-date listing of corrections on our website (ctpub.com). If a correction is not already noted, please contact our customer service department at ctinfo@ctpub.com or P.O. Box 1456, Lafayette, CA 94549.

Trademark (™) and registered trademark (®) names are used throughout this book. Rather than use the symbols with every occurrence of a trademark or registered trademark name, we are using the names only in the editorial fashion and to the benefit of the owner, with no intention of infringement.

Library of Congress Cataloging-in-Publication Data

Names: Brickey, Cheryl, 1978- author.

Title: Just one charm pack quilts : bust your precut stash with 18 projects in 2 colorways / Cheryl Brickey.

Description: Lafayette, CA : C&T Publishing, [2021]

Identifiers: LCCN 2020053402 | ISBN 9781644030844 (trade paperback) | ISBN 9781644030851 (ebook)

Subjects: LCSH: Quilting--Patterns. | Patchwork--Patterns.

Classification: LCC TT835 .B69958 2021 | DDC 746.46/041--dc23

LC record available at https://lccn.loc.gov/2020053402

Printed in the USA

10 9 8 7 6 5

Dedication/Acknowledgments

I would like to thank my wonderful husband, Mike, and my children, Christopher and Sarah, for all of their support (and for tolerating having quilts in various stages of completion all over the house). Thanks also to my official quilt testers—my "herd" of cats—Oreo, Reeses, and Piper.

Many thanks to my parents, Mike and Carole, who gave me my first sewing machine and have always supported me in pursuing my interests and dreams. To all my quilting friends, both local and online, thank you so much for all of your inspiration, friendship, and encouragement.

I would like to thank all my quilting friends that helped with this book by piecing and/or quilting a quilt: Carol Alperin, Michele Blake, Dana Blasi, Delia Dorn, Ruth Freyer, Yvonne Fuchs, Sandra Helsel, Faye Jones, Cindy Kaiser, Valorie Kasten, Cindy Lammon, Cindy Hocker Lange, Darleen Sanford, Travis Seward, Garen Sherwood, and Sarah Snider. A special thank-you goes to Carol Alperin, who did almost all the professional longarming of the quilts in this book.

Many thanks to Robert Kaufman Fabrics, Moda Fabrics, The Warm Company, and Aurifil for their generous donations of fabric, batting, and thread.

Last, and certainly not least, I would like to thank Yvonne Fuchs, for her advice, encouragement, ideas, tech editing, and inspiration. She is one of the most amazing people I have had the pleasure of becoming friends with, and my only regret is not being able to spend enough time with her in person due to living on opposite coasts.

Contents ▪

Projects ▪

Windows 16

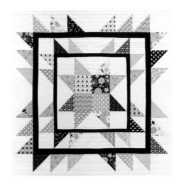

Medallion 23

Fishies 30

Star Surround 38

Ships Ahoy 44

Cat's Eye 50

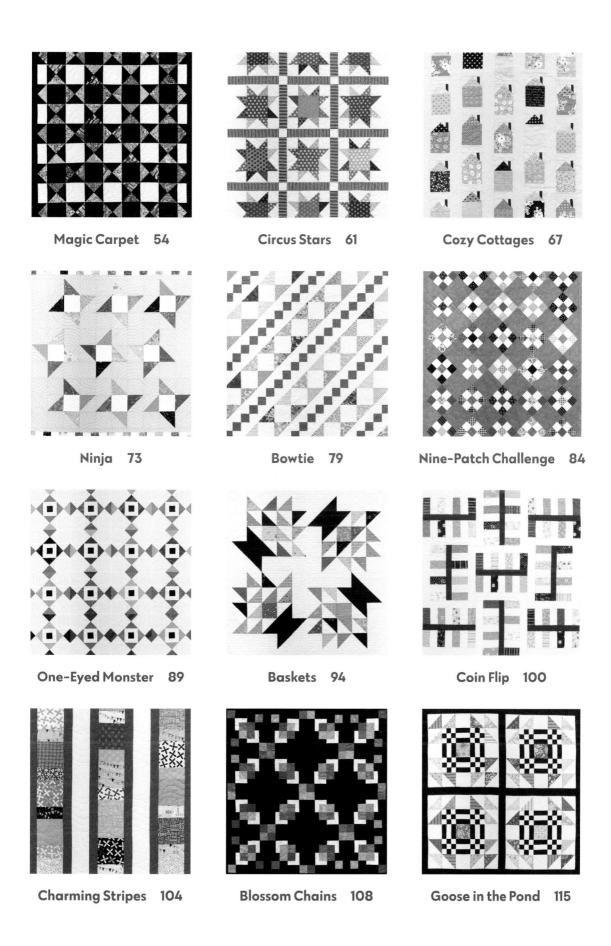

Introduction

Do you have a stack of charm packs in your sewing room? If you are like me, you have numerous charm packs sitting in your sewing room waiting for the perfect project.

Who can resist those little packs when shopping at your local quilt shop or online? When the new fabric collections come out, I often purchase a pack. The packs are inexpensive and a great way to collect a large variety of coordinating prints.

The problem is that whenever I start a new project, the pattern always seems to need multiple charm packs. My stack of charm packs just grows and grows and needs to be put to good use!

Think of this book as the Hamburger Helper of charm packs. Each of the patterns uses just one charm pack along with an additional fabric and background fabric to make a great quilt for a baby, child, table topper, wallhanging, or even a small lap quilt for an adult. You can put your stash of charm packs to good use and create beautiful gifts for friends and loved ones.

All About Charm Packs

Charm packs are curated collections of prints and colors created by a fabric designer or manufacturer. They take the guesswork out of picking fabrics that work well together since the pack usually contains a selection of prints with different scale (large and small scale), print type (floral, stripes, dots, and so on), and colors that all coordinate.

Most charm packs contain 42 squares of 5″ × 5″ fabric, but the quantity included in charm packs varies, so be sure to compare the number of fabric pieces in the charm pack you intend to use with the quilt pattern instructions. Charm packs are also known as 5″ Stackers, Maple Squares, Charm Rolls, or Bali Snaps by different manufacturers.

Newer charm packs can be found in your local quilt shops and online fabric and craft shops. Try searching sites like Etsy and eBay for your favorite designer or brand to see what older packs you can find.

Check the Size

Charm squares are listed as 5″ × 5″ square and usually have pinked edges; pinked edges are cut in a zigzag pattern to help prevent fraying. Before starting to work, check that the charm squares are actually 5″ × 5″ square.

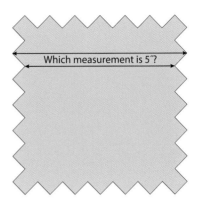

Which measurement is 5″?

For some manufacturers, the 5″ is measured between the tips of the pinked edges, while other manufacturers might measure the 5″ between the valleys of the pinked edges (as shown in the illustration with exaggerated pinked edges). Prior to piecing, taking the time to measure the charm squares to know which measurement is 5″ will save a lot of frustration and time when you begin cutting and piecing blocks together.

tip For example, if the 5″ is measured between the tips of the pinked edges, be sure to align the tips of the charm square with your ruler when cutting or with another fabric when piecing. If the 5″ is measured between the valleys, it might be easiest to trim the charm squares down to a true 5″ square before using them for the best accuracy.

Pick Fabrics from the Pack

Most charm packs contain squares of light, medium, and darker fabrics. Depending on the selected additional and background fabric, you may wish to leave out some of the charm squares that have a low contrast (meaning that they are similar colors) with the additional and/or background fabric. Most of the patterns in this book require between 28–38 charm squares so that it is possible to exclude the low contrast charm squares and still have enough left to make the pattern.

I used the charm pack Lollipop Garden by Lella Boutique for Moda Fabrics in the *Baskets* alternate colorway (next page), which requires 36 charm squares. Prior to piecing, I removed the lighter squares that did not have sufficient contrast with the dark purple (fabric A) and white (background fabric).

Note: All the project quilts are also made in an alternate colorway for inspiration.

Charm squares and fabrics for alternate colorway of *Baskets* (quilt project, page 94; alternate colorway fabric information, page 99)

Add Additional Prints

If, in some cases, you decide to leave out several of your charm prints and find that you do not have enough left to make the pattern, there are four easy fixes:

1. If the charm pack is current and yardage and/or fat quarters are available from the fabric collection, you can buy additional yardage of the chosen prints as and cut the yardage into squares.

2. If the charm pack is older and yardage of the prints are no longer available, try looking at newer lines from the same designer. Many fabric designers' collections are designed to coordinate with past collections, and it may work well to add in some prints from a newer fabric line.

3. Add in some solid fabrics in matching colors. There are hundreds of solid fabric colors available, so it is not difficult to find a couple that coordinate with any charm pack.

4. Shop your stash. Look through your stash and you will most likely be pleasantly surprised to find prints that can supplement the charm pack prints.

In my version of *Cat's Eye* (page 50), I decided to remove the gray prints from the Bonnie & Camille Woven collection because I felt that they were too close to the white background fabric. Once I removed the gray prints, I did not have the 38 prints needed, so I cut a few additional squares out of matching pink and green solid fabrics I already had in my stash.

Make Your Own Charm Pack

You don't need to start with a premade charm pack to make these quilts, you can create your own charm pack!

From Color Inspiration

Pick a color scheme! You can use your favorite colors, like I did with the blue and green prints in the *One-Eyed Monster* (page 89), or you can choose to use all the same type of print such as all plaids or all polka dots.

One way to come up with a color scheme is to find a fabric print you like and then use that to pick fabrics. For the *Magic Carpet* alternate colorway (below), I found an inspiration fabric with colors I really liked from the Waterfront Park collection by Violet Craft for Michael Miller Fabrics. Starting with the Waterfront Park focal fabric, I pulled aqua,

coral, blue, and peach prints that were similar to the focal fabric colors. The additional fabric colors do not need to match exactly; having slight color variations gives the quilt interest. Once I had a large number of fabrics pulled from my stash, I narrowed down my selection of fabrics, while trying to maintain a good mix of colors, scale of prints, types of print, and solids. I suggest cutting no more than 2 or 3 squares 5″ × 5″ of each fabric for the custom charm pack. You can use your inspiration fabric in the quilt top as one of the fabrics or even use it in the backing or binding.

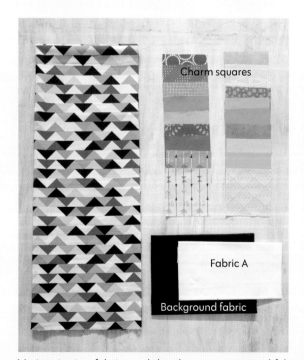 

My inspiration fabric, and the charm squares and fabrics for alternate colorway of *Magic Carpet* (quilt project, page 54; alternate colorway fabric information, page 60)

If you are unsure which colors are in a fabric print, usually the selvage has color spots to aid in color matching.

FABRIC

• *Half-Square Triangle from the Waterfront Park collection by Violet Craft for Michael Miller Fabrics*

From Other Precuts and Yardage

Do you have a lot of scraps, fat quarters, or other yardage?

I like to cut fabric scraps from other patterns into 5″ × 5″ squares and store them together. I also add the extra charm squares from charm packs I did not use in a quilt. You can "shop" this stack of charm squares to create your next quilt.

To cut charm squares from other precuts and yardage:

Precut or yardage	# of charm squares per piece
Precut 10″ squares*	4
Fat quarter (at least 18″ × 20″)	12
½ yard	24

* Sometimes referred to by manufacturer brands, such as Layer Cakes or Stackers.

All About Background Fabric, Additional Fabric, and Binding ■

The background fabric and additional fabric should provide good contrast with the charm square prints.

Background Fabric

The background fabrics should preferably be a solid print or a tone-on-tone or subtle print that reads like a solid from a distance. If large-scale florals or bright gingham prints were used as the background, it would be more difficult to see the quilt design and shapes created by the charm squares.

Additional Fabric *(Fabric A in the Patterns)*

Each of the patterns in the book utilizes an additional fabric (fabric A) in addition to the charm squares and background fabric. This additional fabric helps "stretch" the charm pack enough to make a full quilt and is usually a color and/or print that has enough contrast with both the charm pack fabrics and the background fabric.

To choose the additional fabric, look at the pattern to see if the additional fabric touches the charm squares and/or background fabric. In *Magic Carpet* (page 54), the additional fabric, the background fabric, and the charm squares are all next to each other, so the pattern looks best when there is good contrast between all of them. On

the other hand, in *Cat's Eye* (page 50), the additional fabric is only next to the background fabric (it does not touch any of the charm square) so there is less worry about the contrast between the additional fabric and the charm squares.

One of the prints from the charm pack might work well as the additional fabric, but if your charm pack has been aging like fine wine in your sewing room and the prints from the collection are no longer available, a solid fabric is a great choice. There are so many solid fabric colors available that there is sure to be a color that works well with the charm squares and background fabric.

Binding

The most popular way to finish a quilt is with binding. Binding is a strip of fabric that wraps around and encloses the raw edges of the quilt top. For instructions on how to bind a quilt, see Binding the Quilt (page 121).

Selecting fabric for the binding is a personal preference. I view binding as a frame for the quilt, so I tend to use a binding that is darker than most the quilt, like in *Cat's Eye*. Another option for binding fabric is to use one of the prints from the charm pack, such as in *Ninja* (page 73). I would only caution against using a white or very light binding fabric for a baby or child's quilt as these may show the dirt more easily.

Cat's Eye (page 50) uses a dark blue solid fabric (the same as the fabric A) as the binding.

The binding for *Ninja* (page 73) is the magenta print from the Flower Shop fabric collection.

For most quilts, I do not decide what binding to use until the quilt has been quilted and the batting has been trimmed. Often, the binding I have in mind when I start the quilt does not wind up being my final pick once the quilt is quilted. To audition different fabrics as potential binding fabrics, I place several different fabrics under the edge of the quilt so that they peek out about ½″ from the quilt top to mimic what they would look like as a binding.

tip STRAIGHT GRAIN VERSUS BIAS GRAIN BINDING

The instructions and fabric requirements for the quilts in this book are for straight grain binding, meaning that the strips for the binding are cut from selvage to selvage. Some quilters prefer a bias binding where the strips are cut at a 45° angle to the selvages. If bias binding is your preferred method for binding, additional binding fabric may be required compared to what is listed in the pattern.

Quilt Backings

Make a Backing Bigger

The backings for the quilts in this book are calculated with a 4″ overhang on all sides of the quilt, which makes the backing about 8″ wider and 8″ longer than the quilt top. This overhang is what longarm quilters typically request for quilting. If you are doing the quilting yourself on a domestic quilting machine, you can usually use a smaller overhang and might even be able to get away with a single width backing for several of the quilts.

There are two options in the fabric requirements listed for each quilt backing:

1. Traditional method of using two widths of fabric sewn together and then trimmed. This is the simplest way of sewing a backing, but because most of the book patterns need just over a single width of fabric, this method does use a lot of extra fabric. *fig A*

2. To reduce the amount of excess backing fabric, the second option is to sew a row or column of piecing onto a single width of backing to make it wide enough. This involves a little more sewing, but minimizes the fabric needed for the backing and also makes a more interesting backing.

If the pieced strip is placed along the edge of the backing fabric, there is a danger of some or all of the strip being trimmed off after quilting. If the pieced strip is placed directly in the middle and the backing is not aligned perfectly with the quilt top (which is very difficult to do), the misalignment might be noticeable to the eye.

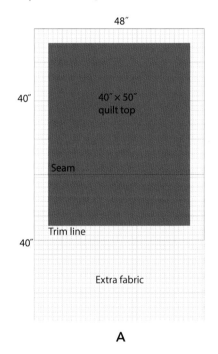

A

For those reasons, I like to place my pieced strip about two-thirds of the way across the quilt backing. This offset uses the rule of thirds (the same rule as in photography for creating interesting photographs) and slight misalignments are less conspicuous. *fig B*

3. Additionally, a wide back fabric (typically 120˝ wide) trimmed to size can also be used, negating the need for any seams.

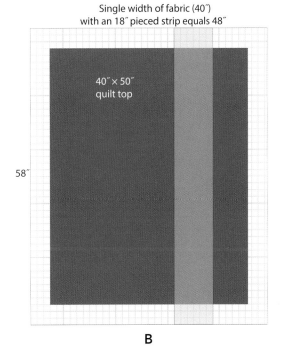

Single width of fabric (40˝)
with an 18˝ pieced strip equals 48˝

40˝ × 50˝
quilt top

58˝

B

Sample Quilt Backs

Here are some backings ideas for inspiration:

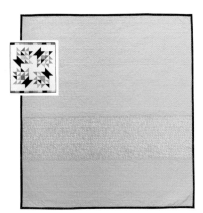

Back of *Baskets* (page 94)

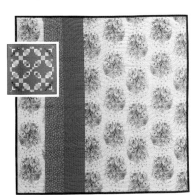

Back of the alternate colorway of *Blossom Chains* (page 108)

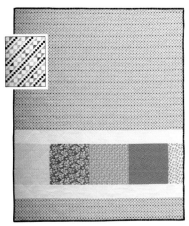

Back of the alternate colorway of *Bowtie* (page 79)

Windows

Pieced by Cheryl Brickey and quilted by Carol Alperin

finished block

5″ × 5″

finished quilt

45½″ × 55½″

social media

#WindowsQuilt

Windows may look like it is pieced on point, but it is really pieced in regular rows and columns with Hourglass blocks between window blocks. The choice of background fabric and fabric A can give the quilt very different looks. In this version of *Windows*, the background fabric is darker than fabric A; while in the alternate colorway version (page 22), the background fabric is lighter than fabric A.

FABRICS USED

- **Charm pack:** *Gooseberry by Vanessa Goertzen from Lella Boutique for Moda Fabrics*
- **Fabric A:** *Bella Solids in White by Moda Fabrics*
- **Background:** *Bella Solids in Steel by Moda Fabrics*

Fabric Requirements

Width of fabric (WOF) is assumed to be at least 40˝.

CHARM SQUARES (5˝ × 5˝): 32

FABRIC A (WHITE): 1¼ yards

BACKGROUND (BG) (GRAY): 2 yards

BINDING (STRAIGHT GRAIN): ½ yard

BACKING: 3 yards
or 1⅞ yards with a 15˝ × 64˝ strip pieced on

BATTING: 54˝ × 64˝

Cutting

CHARM SQUARES

- Cut each charm square in half horizontally and vertically to make 4 charm fabric squares 2½˝ × 2½˝. *Keep the 4 squares cut from each charm square together.*

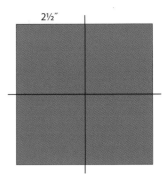

2½˝

FABRIC A (WHITE)

- Cut 4 strips 6½˝ × WOF.

  Subcut the strips into 21 squares 6½˝ × 6½˝ (each strip can yield 6 squares).

- Cut 6 strips 1½˝ × WOF.

  Subcut 3 strips into 40 rectangles 1½˝ × 2½˝ (each strip can yield 16 rectangles).

  Subcut 3 strips into 20 rectangles 1½˝ × 5½˝ (each strip can yield 7 rectangles).

BACKGROUND (BG) (GRAY)

- Cut 4 strips 6½˝ × WOF.

  Subcut the strips into 21 squares 6½˝ × 6½˝ (each strip can yield 6 squares).

- Cut 2 strips 6˝ × WOF.

  Subcut the strips into 9 squares 6˝ × 6˝ (each strip can yield 6 squares).

- Cut 3 strips 5½˝ × WOF.

  Subcut the strips into 18 squares 5½˝ × 5½˝ (each strip can yield 7 squares).

- Cut 4 strips 1½˝ × WOF.

  Subcut 2 strips into 24 rectangles 1½˝ × 2½˝ (each strip can yield 16 rectangles).

  Subcut 2 strips into 12 rectangles 1½˝ × 5½˝ (each strip can yield 7 rectangles).

BINDING

- Cut 6 strips 2½˝ × WOF.

Piecing the Unit and Blocks

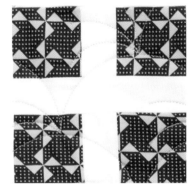

Use a scant ¼˝ (a thread width smaller than ¼˝) seam throughout the construction of the quilt top unless otherwise instructed.

Window Blocks

Make 20 fabric A window blocks and 12 background fabric window blocks.

1. Arrange the following pieces as shown:

- 4 matching charm fabric squares 2½˝ × 2½˝
- 2 fabric A rectangles 1½˝ × 2½˝
- 1 fabric A rectangle 1½˝ × 5½˝

2. Sew the rows together, pressing the seams open or toward the top and bottom pieced rows, to make a fabric A window block 5½˝ × 5½˝.

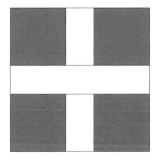

3. Repeat Steps 1 and 2 to make a total of 20 fabric A window blocks.

4. Repeat Steps 1 and 2 using bg rectangles instead of the fabric A rectangles to make a total of 12 bg window blocks 5½˝ × 5½˝ (5˝ × 5˝ in the finished quilt top).

- 4 matching charm fabric squares 2½˝ × 2½˝
- 2 bg rectangles 1½˝ × 2½˝
- 1 bg rectangle 1½˝ × 5½˝

Half-Square Triangle (HST) Units

1. Place a fabric A square 6½″ × 6½″ and a bg square 6½″ × 6½″ right sides together. Draw a diagonal line using a removable marking device on the back of the lighter square (shown as the solid line).

2. Sew a ¼″ seam on both sides of the solid line (shown as the dotted lines). Cut on the solid line and press the seam open or toward the darker fabric.

3. Repeat Steps 1 and 2 to make a total of 42 HST units approximately 6″ × 6″ (41 will be used in the quilt). *Do not trim the HST units as they will be used to make the Hourglass and half-Hourglass blocks.*

 =

Full Hourglass Blocks

1. Place 2 HST units approximately 6″ × 6″ right sides together such that the seams nest together and HST units are oriented as shown in the illustration.

2. Draw a diagonal line using a removable marking device on the back of the one of the HST units (shown as the solid line) perpendicular to the seam of that HST unit.

3. Sew a ¼″ seam on each side of the solid line (shown as the dotted lines). Cut on the solid line and press the seams open.

4. Trim full Hourglass blocks to 5½″ × 5½″. *Each set of 2 HST units will yield 2 full Hourglass blocks.*

5. Repeat Steps 1–4 to make a total of 32 full Hourglass blocks 5½″ × 5½″ (31 will be used in the quilt).

 =

Half-Hourglass Blocks

1. Place a HST unit approximately 6″ × 6″ and a bg square 6″ × 6″ right sides together.

2. Draw a diagonal line using a removable marking device on the back of the HST unit (shown as the solid line) perpendicular to the seam of the HST unit.

3. Sew a ¼″ seam on each side of the solid line (shown as the dotted lines). Cut on the solid line and press the seams open.

4. Trim half-Hourglass blocks to 5½″ × 5½″. *Each set of 1 HST unit and 1 bg square will yield 2 half-Hourglass blocks.*

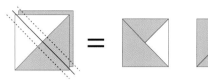

5. Repeat Steps 1–4 to make a total of 18 half-Hourglass blocks 5½″ × 5½″.

Quilt Top Assembly

Row A

1. Sew together the following blocks and pieces, pressing the seams open or toward the bg squares to make a row A 5½″ × 45½″. *The seam direction in the half-Hourglass blocks does not matter.*

- 4 half-Hourglass blocks 5½″ × 5½″
- 5 bg squares 5½″ × 5½″

2. Repeat Step 1 to make a total of 2 row A.

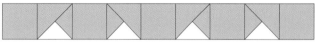

Row A

Row B

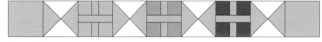

Row C

Row B

1. Sew together the following blocks and pieces, pressing the seams open or toward the window blocks to make a row B 5½″ × 45½″. *The seam direction in the half-Hourglass blocks does not matter.*

- 4 fabric A window blocks 5½″ × 5½″
- 3 full Hourglass blocks 5½″ × 5½″
- 2 half-Hourglass blocks 5½″ × 5½″

2. Repeat Step 1 to make a total of 5 row B.

Row C

1. Sew together the following blocks and pieces, pressing the seams open or toward the window blocks and bg squares to make a row C 5½″ × 45½″.

- 3 bg window blocks 5½″ × 5½″
- 4 full Hourglass blocks 5½″ × 5½″
- 2 bg squares 5½″ × 5½″

2. Repeat Step 1 to make a total of 4 row C.

Piece Quilt Top

Sew together the following rows as shown in the quilt top diagram, pressing the seams open. The quilt top should measure 45½″ × 55½″.

- 2 row A
- 5 row B
- 4 row C

Finishing

For complete instructions, refer to Finishing the Quilt (page 121).

1. Make the quilt backing:

- Remove the selvages. Cut the fabric into 2 pieces (about 54″ × WOF), and sew the backing pieces together along the trimmed selvage edges, using a ½″ seam. Press the seam open. Trim to approximately 54″ × 64″.

  or

- Sew a 15″ × 64″ strip onto a 64″ × WOF piece of fabric to make a 54″ × 64″ backing.

2. Layer the quilt top, batting, and backing. Baste and quilt as desired. *Windows* was quilted in a clamshell design.

3. Bind and enjoy your quilt!

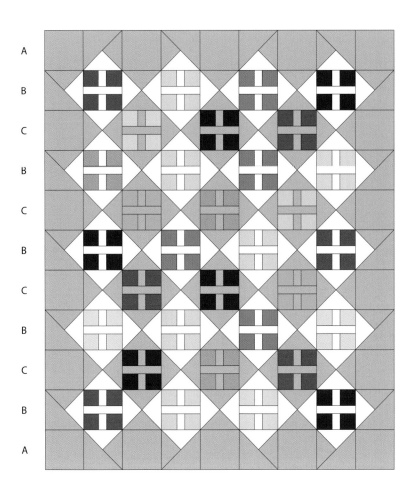

A
B
C
B
C
B
C
B
C
B
A

alternate colorway

Pieced and quilted by Sandra Helsel

FABRICS USED

- **Charm pack:** *Marmalade by Bonnie & Camille for Moda Fabrics*
- **Fabric A:** *Bella Solids in Natural by Moda Fabrics*
- **Background:** *Bella Solids in White by Moda Fabrics*

Medallion

Pieced and quilted
by Dana Blasi

finished quilt

39½″ × 39½″

social media

#MedallionQuilt

This vibrant medallion-style quilt features blocks added in a series of borders. The exploding star design makes a lovely wallhanging or even a table quilt or small lap quilt.

Fabric Requirements

Width of fabric (WOF) is assumed to be at least 40˝.

CHARM SQUARES (5˝ × 5˝): 36

FABRIC A (BLUE): ⅜ yard

BACKGROUND (BG) (WHITE): 1⅜ yards

BINDING (STRAIGHT GRAIN): ½ yard

BACKING: 2⅔ yards or 1⅓ yards with a 9˝ × 48˝ strip pieced on

BATTING: 48˝ × 48˝

Cutting

CHARM SQUARES

- Trim 12 charm squares to 4½˝ × 4½˝.

- The remaining 24 charm squares will be used as 5˝ × 5˝ squares.

FABRIC A (BLUE)

- Cut 4 strips 1¾˝ × WOF.

  Subcut 2 strips each into 1 piece 1¾˝ × 25˝.
  Subcut 2 strips each into 1 piece 1¾˝ × 27½˝.

- Cut 2 strips 1¼˝ × WOF.

  Subcut 1 strip into 2 pieces 1¼˝ × 18˝.
  Subcut 1 strip into 2 pieces 1¼˝ × 16½˝.

BACKGROUND (BG) (WHITE)

- Cut 3 strips 5˝ × WOF.

  Subcut the strips into 24 squares 5˝ × 5˝ (each strip can yield 8 squares).

- Cut 3 strips 4½˝ × WOF.

  Subcut 1 strip into 4 rectangles 4½˝ × 8½˝.
  Subcut 1 strip into 8 squares 4½˝ × 4½˝.
  Subcut 1 strip into 4 rectangles 4½˝ × 3½˝.

- Cut 1 strip 4˝ × WOF.

  Subcut the strip into 8 squares 4˝ × 4˝.

- Cut 4 strips 2½˝ × WOF.

  Subcut 2 strips each into 1 piece 2½˝ × 39½˝.
  Subcut 2 strips each into 1 piece 2½˝ × 35½˝.

BINDING

- Cut 5 strips 2½˝ × WOF.

FABRICS USED

- **Charm pack:** Azure Skies by Simple Simon & Company for Riley Blake Designs
- **Fabric A**: Bella Solids in Nautical Blue by Moda Fabrics
- **Background:** Bella Solids in White by Moda Fabrics

Piecing the Units and Block

Use a scant ¼˝ (a thread width smaller than ¼˝) seam throughout the construction of the quilt top unless otherwise instructed.

Half-Square Triangle (HST) Units

1. Place a charm square 5˝ × 5˝ and a bg square 5˝ × 5˝ right sides together. Draw a diagonal line using a removable marking device on the back of the lighter square (shown as the solid line).

2. Sew a ¼˝ seam on both sides of the solid line (shown as the dotted lines). Cut on the solid line and press the seam open or toward the darker fabric.

3. From each pair of HST units, trim 1 HST unit to 4½˝ × 4½˝ and 1 HST unit to 4˝ × 4˝.

4. Repeat Steps 1–3 to make a total of 24 large HST units 4½˝ × 4½˝ and 24 small HST units 4˝ × 4˝ (only 16 of the small HST units are used in the quilt top).

Flying Geese Units

1. Place a charm fabric square 4½˝ × 4½˝ on one side of a bg rectangle 4½˝ × 8½˝ right sides together.

Draw a diagonal line on the back of the charm fabric square using a removable marking device and sew on the marked line (shown as the dotted line).

Trim a ¼˝ from the stitched line and the press the seam open or toward the darker fabric.

2. Place a charm fabric square 4½˝ × 4½˝ (with a different print) on the opposite end of the bg rectangle and sew together as in Step 1.

3. Trim Flying Geese unit to 4½˝ × 8½˝ if necessary, making sure there is ¼˝ between the point of the bg triangle and the edge of the unit.

4. Repeat Steps 1–3 to make a total of 4 Flying Geese units 4½˝ × 8½˝.

Center Block

1. Sew together 4 charm fabric squares 4½˝ × 4½˝, pressing the seams open, to make a center unit 8½˝ × 8½˝.

2. Arrange the following units and pieces according to the diagram:

- 1 center unit 8½˝ × 8½˝
- 4 Flying Geese units 4½˝ × 8½˝
- 4 bg squares 4½˝ × 4½˝

3. Sew the units and pieces into rows, pressing the seams open or away from the Flying Geese units.

4. Sew the rows together, pressing the seams open, to make the center block 16½˝ × 16½˝.

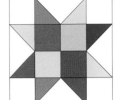

Quilt Top Assembly

Press all seams open during construction of the quilt top.

First Border

1. Sew a fabric A piece 1¼˝ × 16½˝ onto both sides of the center block.

2. Sew a fabric A piece 1¼˝ × 18˝ onto the top and bottom of center block. The quilt top should measure 18˝ × 18˝.

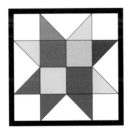

Second Border

1. Sew together 4 small HST 4˝ × 4˝ and 1 bg square 4˝ × 4˝ to make a side border 4˝ × 18˝.

2. Repeat Step 1 to make a total of 2 side borders.

3. Sew the side borders onto the sides of the quilt top.

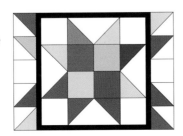

4. Sew together 4 small HST 4˝ × 4˝ and 3 bg squares 4˝ × 4˝ to make a top/bottom border 4˝ × 25˝ as shown.

5. Repeat Step 4 to make a total of 2 top/bottom borders.

6. Sew the top/bottom borders onto the top and bottom of the quilt top. The quilt top should measure 25˝ × 25˝.

Third Border

1. Sew a fabric A piece 1¾″ × 25″ onto both sides of the center block.

2. Sew a fabric A piece 1¾″ × 27½″ onto the top and bottom of center block. The quilt top, after the third border layer is added, should measure 27½″ × 27½″.

Fourth Border

1. Sew together 6 large HST 4½″ × 4½″ and 1 bg rectangle 3½″ × 4½″ as shown, to make a side border 4½″ × 27½″.

2. Repeat Step 1 to make a total of 2 side borders.

3. Sew the side borders onto the sides of the quilt top.

4. Sew together 6 large HST 4½″ × 4½″, 2 bg squares 4½″ × 4½″, and 1 bg rectangle 3½″ × 4½″ to make a top/bottom border 4½″ × 35½″ as shown.

5. Repeat Step 4 to make a total of 2 top/bottom borders.

6. Sew the top/bottom borders onto the top and bottom of the quilt top. The quilt top, after the fourth border layer is added, should measure 35½″ × 35½″.

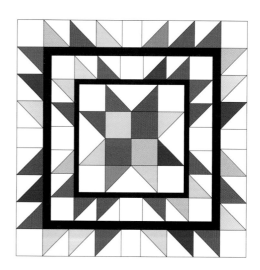

Fifth Border

1. Sew a bg piece 2½″ × 35½″ onto both sides of the center block.

2. Sew a bg piece 2½″ × 39½″ onto the top and bottom of center block. The finished quilt top, after the fifth and final border layer is added, should measure 39½″ × 39½″.

Finishing

For complete instructions, refer to Finishing the Quilt (page 121).

1. Make the quilt backing:

- Remove the selvages. Cut the fabric into 2 pieces (about 48″ × WOF), and sew the backing pieces together along the trimmed selvage edges, using a ½″ seam. Press the seam open. Trim to approximately 48″ × 48″.

or

- Sew a 9″ × 48″ strip onto a 48″ × WOF piece of fabric to make a 48″ × 48″ backing.

2. Layer the quilt top, batting, and backing. Baste and quilt as desired. *Medallion* was quilted with serpentine lines.

3. Bind and enjoy your quilt!

alternate colorway

Pieced and quilted by Cheryl Brickey

FABRICS USED

- ***Charm pack:*** *Spellbound by Urban Chiks for Moda Fabrics*

- ***Fabric A:*** *Bella Solids in White by Moda Fabrics*

- ***Background:*** *Bella Solids in Black by Moda Fabrics*

Fishies

Pieced by Cheryl Brickey and quilted by Carol Alperin

finished block

4″ × 4″

finished quilt

43½″ × 48½″

social media

#FishiesQuilt

Schools of fishies are swimming across the *Fishies* quilt. I love the Breeze charm pack prints which contained pinks, blues, and navy prints. I bought two packs, then used the blue prints for *Fishies* and the pink and navy prints for the *Cozy Cottages* alternate colorway (page 72).

FABRICS USED

- **Charm pack:** Breeze by Zen Chic for Moda Fabrics
- **Fabric A:** Dottie Circles in Azure from the Breeze collection by Zen Chic for Moda Fabrics
- **Background:** Bella Solids in Navy by Moda Fabrics

tips FOR SEWING BIAS SEAMS

Fishies is one of the more challenging patterns in the book due to the bias seams within the fish blocks. Here are some tips for successful bias seam sewing:

- Starch your fabrics before cutting them. This makes the fabric stiffer and the bias edges less likely to warp or stretch.

- Take care not to stretch the triangles when sewing the bias edges together.

- Press the seams (lifting the iron straight up and down) instead of ironing.

Fabric Requirements

Width of fabric (WOF) is assumed to be at least 40˝.

CHARM SQUARES (5˝ × 5˝): 32

FABRIC A (LIGHT BLUE):
⅜ yard

BACKGROUND (BG) (NAVY):
1⅞ yards

BINDING (STRAIGHT GRAIN):
½ yard

BACKING: 2⅞ yards
or 1⅝ yards with a
13˝ × 57˝ strip pieced on

BATTING: 52˝ × 57˝

Cutting

CHARM SQUARES

Cut each charm square into 1 triangle 4⅞˝ × 4⅞˝ and 1 triangle 2⅞˝ × 2⅞˝.

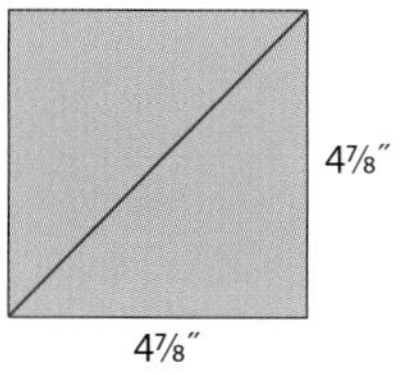

1. Trim the charm square to 4⅞˝ × 4⅞˝.

2. Cut the charm fabric square in half on the diagonal (red line) to make 2 triangles 4⅞˝ × 4⅞˝.

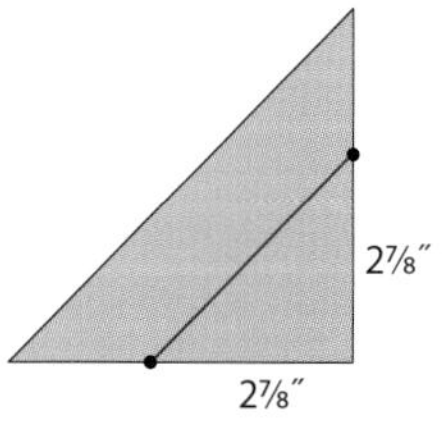

3. From 1 triangle from Step 2, measure and mark 2⅞˝ × 2⅞˝ from the corner on both sides (black dots), then draw a line connecting the markings (red line).

4. Cut on the marked line to make 1 triangle 2⅞˝ × 2⅞˝. (The remainder of the charm fabric square may be discarded or added to your scrap basket.)

FABRIC A (LIGHT BLUE)

- Cut 5 strips 2˝ × WOF for second border.

BACKGROUND (BG) (NAVY)

- Cut 1 strip 6½″ × WOF.

  Subcut the strip into 2 rectangles 6½″ × 16½″.

- Cut 5 strips 4½″ × WOF.

  Subcut 2 strips each into 2 rectangles 4½″ × 12½″ and 1 rectangle 4½″ × 8½″. From the remainder of 1 strip, cut 1 rectangle 3½″ × 6″.

  Subcut 1 strip into 2 rectangles 4½″ × 8½″ and 4 squares 4½″ × 4½″.

  Subcut 2 strips into 24 rectangles 4½″ × 2½″ (each strip can yield 16 rectangles).

- Cut 1 strip 3½″ × WOF for center strip.

- Cut 4 strips 2⅞″ × WOF.

  Subcut the strips into 48 squares 2⅞″ × 2⅞″ (each strip can yield 13 squares). Cut each square 2⅞″ × 2⅞″ in half once on diagonal to make 96 triangles 2⅞″ × 2⅞″.

- Cut 5 strips 3″ × WOF for first border.

BINDING

- Cut 5 strips 2½″ × WOF.

Piecing the Block

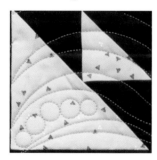

Use a scant ¼″ (a thread width smaller than ¼″) seam throughout the construction of the quilt top unless otherwise instructed.

Fish Blocks

Press all seams open during the construction of the fish blocks.

1. Gather matching charm fabric triangles within each block and each block uses:

- 1 charm fabric triangle 4⅞″ × 4⅞″
- 1 charm fabric triangle 2⅞″ × 2⅞″
- 3 bg triangles 2⅞″ × 2⅞″

2. Sew together a charm fabric triangle 2⅞″ × 2⅞″ and a bg triangle 2⅞″ × 2⅞″ to make a half-square triangle (HST). Trim the dog-ears off the units (little tabs of fabric that extend past the unit).

3. Sew 2 bg triangles 2⅞″ × 2⅞″ onto the HST. *Make sure the orientations of the bg triangles relative to the HST match the illustration.*

4. Sew together the unit from Step 3 with a charm fabric triangle 4⅞″ × 4⅞″ to make a fish block 4½″ × 4½″.

5. Repeat Steps 2–4 to make a total of 32 fish blocks 4½″ × 4½″ (4″ × 4″ in the finished quilt top).

Piecing the Sections

Fish Sections

1. Arrange the following fish blocks and pieces as shown.

- 4 fish blocks 4½″ × 4½″
- 3 bg rectangles 2½″ × 4½″

2. Sew together the fish blocks and pieces with the fish pointing to the lower left corner of the blocks, pressing the seams open or toward the bg rectangles, to make a first fish section 4½″ × 22½″.

3. Repeat Steps 1 and 2 to make a total of 4 first fish sections 4½″ × 22½″. fig A

4. Repeat Steps 1 and 2 with the fish blocks pointing to the upper left corner to make a total of 4 second fish sections 4½″ × 22½″. *The second fish section is a mirror image of the first fish section. fig B*

A   B

Left Side of Quilt

1. Following the left side of quilt top diagrams, arrange the following sections and pieces:

- 4 first fish sections 4½″ × 22½″
- 2 bg rectangle 4½″ × 12½″
- 2 bg rectangles 4½″ × 8½″
- 2 bg squares 4½″ × 4½″

2. Sew the sections and pieces into columns, then sew the columns together, pressing the seams open.

3. Sew 1 bg rectangle 6½″ × 16½″ on the bottom of the section from Step 2, pressing the seam open, to make the left side of the quilt top 16½″ × 40½″. *fig C*

Right Side of Quilt

1. Following the right side of quilt top diagrams, arrange the following sections and pieces:

- 4 second fish sections 4½″ × 22½″
- 2 bg rectangle 4½″ × 12½″
- 2 bg rectangles 4½″ × 8½″
- 2 bg squares 4½″ × 4½″

2. Sew the sections and pieces into columns, then sew columns together, pressing the seams open.

3. Sew 1 bg rectangle 6½″ × 16½″ on the top of the section from Step 2, pressing the seam open, to make the right side of the quilt top 16½″ × 40½″. *fig D*

Center Strip

Sew the center strip. If your fabric has a WOF of 40½″ or greater, then you only need a single strip. If your fabric has a WOF of less than 40½″ than sew together the bg strip 3½″ × WOF and the bg rectangle 3½″ × 6″ and trim to 40½″ to make the center strip. The center strip should measure 3½″ × 40½″.

C

D

Quilt Top Assembly

Sew together the left side of the quilt top, the center strip, and the right side of the quilt top and press the seams open. The quilt top, before borders are added, should measure 35½″ × 40½″.

Left of quilt top   Center strip   Right of quilt top

First Border

Some fabrics have a width of fabric (WOF) wider than the 40″ assumed by this pattern. If your fabric has a WOF of at least 40½″, then you do not need to piece your fabric for the first border.

1. Cut 1 bg strip 3″ × WOF into 4 pieces (3″ × about 10″) and sew each bg piece 3″ × about 10″ to a full bg strip 3″ × WOF.

2. Trim 2 of the pieced bg strips to the average height of the quilt top, approximately 40½″, and sew onto the sides of the quilt, pressing the seams open or toward the borders.

3. Trim 2 of the pieced bg strips to the average width of the quilt top, approximately 40½″, and sew onto the top and bottom of the quilt, pressing the seams open or toward the borders. The quilt top with the first border should measure 40½″ × 45½″.

Second Border

1. Cut 1 fabric A border strip 2″ × WOF into 4 pieces (2″ × about 10″) and sew each piece 2″ × about 10″ to a full border strip 2″ × WOF.

2. Trim 2 of the pieced border strips to the average height of the quilt top, approximately 45½″ and sew onto the sides of the quilt, pressing the seams open or toward the borders.

3. Trim 2 of the pieced bg strips to the average width of the quilt top, approximately 43½″ and sew onto the top and bottom of the quilt, pressing the seams open or toward the borders. The finished quilt top should measure approximately 43½″ × 48½″.

Finishing

For complete instructions, refer to Finishing the Quilt (page 121).

1. Make the quilt backing:

- Remove the selvages. Cut the fabric into 2 pieces (about 52″ × WOF), and sew the backing pieces together along the trimmed selvage edges, using a ½″ seam. Press the seam open. Trim to approximately 52″ × 57″.

  or

- Sew a 13″ × 57″ strip onto a 57″ × WOF piece of fabric to make a 52″ × 57″ backing.

2. Layer the quilt top, batting, and backing. Baste and quilt as desired. *Fishies* was quilted in an ocean wave design.

3. Bind and enjoy your quilt!

alternate colorway

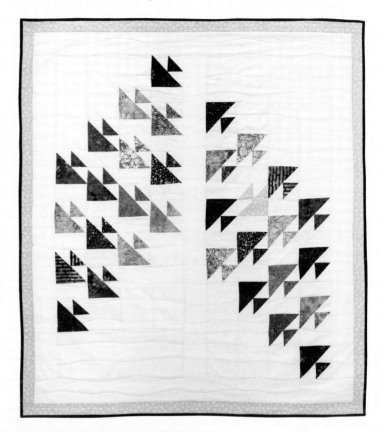

Pieced and quilted by Faye Jones

For a little twist on the Fishies pattern, Faye made one of her fish blocks using her fabric A and then turned the fish around so that it was swimming through the school of fish.

FABRICS USED

- **Charm pack:** *High Tide Batiks by Bluprint*
- **Fabric A:** *Hash Dot in Grass by Michael Miller Fabrics*
- **Background:** *Bella Solids in Tranquil Aqua by Moda Fabrics*

Star Surround

Pieced by Cheryl Brickey and quilted by Carol Alperin

finished block
16″ × 16″

finished quilt
51½″ × 51½″

social media
#StarSurroundQuilt

Most charm packs contain an assortment of coordinating prints, but there are also a wide variety of solid fabric charm packs available like the Sunset Palette charm pack. For this pattern, I excluded some of the charm squares that I felt did not have enough contrast with the dark purple fabric A.

FABRICS USED

- **Charm pack:** *Sunset Palette of Kona Cotton Solids by Robert Kaufman Fabrics*
- **Fabric A:** *Kona Cotton Solids in Hibiscus by Robert Kaufman Fabrics*
- **Background:** *Kona Cotton Solids in Thistle by Robert Kaufman Fabrics*

Fabric Requirements

Width of fabric (WOF) is assumed to be at least 40″.

CHARM SQUARES (5″ × 5″): 28

FABRIC A (DARK PURPLE): 1⅛ yards

BACKGROUND (BG) (LIGHT PURPLE): 2½ yards

BINDING (STRAIGHT GRAIN): ½ yard

BACKING: 3⅓ yards or 1⅔ yards with a 20″ × 60″ strip pieced on

BATTING: 60″ × 60″

Cutting

CHARM SQUARES

- Trim each charm square to 4½″ × 4½″.

FABRIC A (DARK PURPLE)

- Cut 7 strips 4½″ × WOF.

  Subcut the strips into 56 squares 4½″ × 4½″ (each strip can yield 8 squares).

BACKGROUND (BG) (LIGHT PURPLE)

- Cut 2 strips 8½″ × WOF.

  Subcut the strips into 4 rectangles 8½″ × 16½″ (each strip can yield 2 rectangles).

- Cut 11 strips 4½″ × WOF.

  Subcut 7 strips into 28 rectangles 4½″ × 8½″ (each strip can yield 4 rectangles).

  Subcut 4 strips into 28 squares 4½″ × 4½″ (each strip can yield 8 squares).

- Cut 6 strips 2″ × WOF for borders.

BINDING

- Cut 6 strips 2½″ × WOF.

Piecing Units and Blocks

Use a scant ¼″ (a thread width smaller than ¼″) seam throughout the construction of the quilt top unless otherwise instructed.

Flying Geese Units

1. Place a fabric A square 4½˝ × 4½˝ on one side of a bg rectangle 4½˝ × 8½˝ right sides together.

Draw a diagonal line on the back of the fabric A square using a removable marking device and sew on the marked line (shown as the dotted line).

Trim a ¼˝ from the stitched line and press the seam open or toward the darker fabric.

2. Place a fabric A square 4½˝ × 4½˝ on the opposite end of the bg rectangle and sew together as in Step 1.

3. Trim Flying Geese unit to 4½˝ × 8½˝ if necessary, making sure there is ¼˝ between the point of the bg triangle and the edge of the unit.

4. Repeat Steps 1–3 to make a total of 28 Flying Geese units 4½˝ × 8½˝.

Center Units

1. Sew together 4 charm squares 4½˝ × 4½˝, pressing the seams open, to make a center unit 8½˝ × 8½˝.

2. Repeat Step 2 to make a total of 7 center units.

Center Blocks

1. Arrange the following units and pieces according to the diagram:

- 1 center unit 8½˝ × 8½˝
- 4 Flying Geese units 4½˝ × 8½˝
- 4 bg squares 4½˝ × 4½˝

2. Sew the units and pieces into rows, pressing the seams open or away from the Flying Geese units.

3. Sew the rows together, pressing the seams open, to make a star block 16½˝ × 16½˝.

4. Repeat Steps 1–3 to make a total of 7 star blocks 16½˝ × 16½˝ (16˝ × 16˝ in the finished quilt top).

Quilt Top Assembly

Column A

1. Sew together 2 star blocks 16½″ × 16½″ and 2 bg rectangles 8½″ × 16½″, pressing the seams open, to make a column A 16½″ × 48½″. fig A

2. Repeat Step 1 to make a total of 2 column A.

Column B

Sew together 3 star blocks 16½″ × 16½″, pressing the seams open, to make a column B 16½″ × 48½″. fig B

Piece Quilt Top

Sew the 2 column A and 1 column B together, pressing the seams open. The quilt top, before borders are added, should measure 48½″ × 48½″.

Borders

1. Cut 1 bg strip 2″ × WOF in half and sew each half to a full bg strip 2″ × WOF. Trim to the average height of the quilt, approximately 48½″. Sew the borders onto the sides of the quilt top, pressing the seams open or toward the borders.

2. Cut 1 bg strip 2″ × WOF in half and sew each half to a full bg strip 2″ × WOF. Trim to the average width of the quilt, approximately 51½″. Sew the borders onto the top and bottom of the quilt top, pressing the seams open or toward the borders. The quilt top should measure approximately 51½″ × 51½″.

A   B

A   B   A

Finishing

For complete instructions, refer to Finishing the Quilt (page 121).

1. Make the quilt backing:

- Remove the selvages. Cut the fabric into 2 pieces (about 60″ × WOF), and sew the backing pieces together along the trimmed selvage edges, using a ½″ seam. Press the seam open. Trim to approximately 60″ × 60″.

  or

- Sew a 20″ × 60″ strip onto a 60″ × WOF piece of fabric to make a 60″ × 60″ backing.

2. Layer the quilt top, batting, and backing. Baste and quilt as desired. *Star Surround* was quilted in a swirl design.

3. Bind and enjoy your quilt!

alternate colorway

Pieced by Cheryl Brickey and quilted by Carol Alperin

FABRICS USED

- **Charm pack:** *Fruta y Flor by Verna Mosquera for FreeSpirit Fabrics*
- **Fabric A:** *Bella Solids in White by Moda Fabrics*
- **Background:** *FreeSpirit Solids in Pomegranate by FreeSpirit Fabrics*

Ships Ahoy

Pieced by Cheryl Brickey and quilted by Carol Alperin

finished block
12½˝ × 12½˝

finished quilt
45˝ × 50˝

social media
#ShipsAhoyQuilt

Ships Ahoy earned its name from the combination of the lifesaver ring–like blocks and the nautical fabric. The alternate colorway version uses softer colors and floral prints, which give the quilt a very different look.

FABRICS USED

- **Charm pack:** Daysail by Bonnie & Camille for Moda Fabrics

- **Fabric A:** Bella Solids in Navy by Moda Fabrics

- **Background:** Bella Solids in White by Moda Fabrics

Fabric Requirements

Width of fabric (WOF) is assumed to be at least 40˝.

CHARM SQUARES (5˝ × 5˝): 36

FABRIC A (NAVY): 1 yard

BACKGROUND (BG) (WHITE): 1½ yards

BINDING (STRAIGHT GRAIN): ½ yard

BACKING: 3 yards or 1⅝ yards with a 14˝ × 58˝ strip pieced on

BATTING: 53˝ × 58˝

Cutting

tip OVERSIZING TRIANGLES FOR SQUARE-IN-A-SQUARE (SIAS) BLOCKS
Oversizing triangles sewn onto the inner square in the SiaS and then trimming the finished block down to size makes sewing the blocks easier and more accurate. If you'd like to oversize your triangles, cut fabric A and bg squares to 4¼˝ × 4¼˝ instead of 3¾˝ × 3¾˝.

CHARM SQUARES

- Trim each charm square to 4½˝ × 4½˝.

FABRIC A (NAVY)

- Cut 4 strips 3¾˝ × WOF.

  Subcut the strips into 36 squares 3¾˝ × 3¾˝ (each strip can yield 10 squares). Cut each square once on the diagonal to make 72 triangles 3¾˝ × 3¾˝.

- Cut 3 strips 3˝ × WOF for second border.

BACKGROUND (BG) (TEAL)

- Cut 4 strips 3¾˝ × WOF.

  Subcut the strips into 36 squares 3¾˝ × 3¾˝ (each strip can yield 10 squares). Cut each square once on the diagonal to make 72 triangles 3¾˝ × 3¾˝.

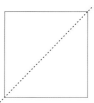

- Cut 5 strips 2½˝ × WOF.

  Subcut 2 strips into 6 rectangles 2½˝ × 13˝ (each strip can yield 3 rectangles). Reserve 3 strips for sashing.

- Cut 5 strips 2˝ × WOF for first border.

- Cut 6 strips 1½˝ × WOF.

  Subcut 3 strips into 18 rectangles 1½˝ × 6¼˝ (each strip can yield 6 rectangles).

  Subcut 3 strips into 9 rectangles 1½˝ × 13˝ (each strip can yield 3 rectangles).

BINDING

- Cut 5 strips 2½˝ × WOF.

Piecing the Unit and Block

Use a scant ¼˝ (a thread width smaller than ¼˝) seam throughout the construction of the quilt top unless otherwise instructed.

Square-in-a-Square (SiaS) Units

1. Center a fabric A triangle 3¾˝ × 3¾˝ along a first side of a charm fabric square 4½˝ × 4½˝. Sew along the edge (seam shown as a dotted line), pressing the seam open or outward.

2. Sew a second fabric A triangle 3¾˝ × 3¾˝ on the opposite side of the charm fabric square, pressing the seam open or outward. *Both of these triangles can be sewn on and then pressed instead of pressing after each addition.*

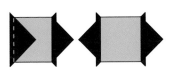

3. Continue by sewing 2 bg triangles 3¾˝ × 3¾˝ onto the other 2 sides of the square, pressing the seams open or outward.

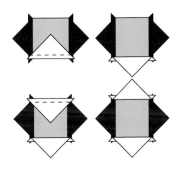

4. Trim off the dog-ears formed by the sewn on triangles and square the unit to 6¼˝ × 6¼˝ (if necessary), making sure there is ¼˝ between the corner of the inner square and the outer side of the unit.

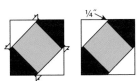

5. Repeat Steps 1–4 to make a total of 36 square-in-a-square (SiaS) units 6¼˝ × 6¼˝.

Block Assembly

1. Arrange the following units and pieces according to the diagram:

- 4 SiaS units 6¼˝ × 6¼˝
- 2 bg rectangles 1½˝ × 6¼˝
- 1 bg rectangle 1½˝ × 13˝

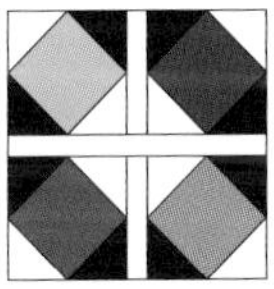

2. Sew the units and pieces into rows, pressing the seams open or toward the bg rectangles. Sew the rows together, pressing the seams open or toward the bg rectangles, to make a block 13˝ × 13˝ (12½˝ × 12½˝ in the finished quilt top).

3. Repeat Steps 1 and 2 to make a total of 9 blocks.

Quilt Top Assembly

Block Rows

1. Sew together 3 blocks 13˝ × 13˝ and 2 bg rectangles 2½˝ × 13˝, pressing the seams open or away from the blocks, to make a block row 13˝ × 42˝.

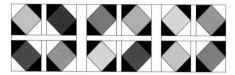

2. Repeat Step 1 to make a total of 3 block rows.

Sashing Rows

Cut 1 bg strip 2½˝ × WOF in half, sew each half to a full bg strip 2½˝ × WOF, and trim to 42˝ to make 2 sashing rows 2½˝ × 42˝.

Piece Quilt Top

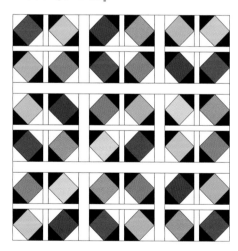

Sew together 3 block rows 13˝ × 42˝ and 2 sashing rows 2½˝ × 42˝, pressing the seams open. The quilt top, before borders are added, should measure 42˝ × 42˝.

Borders

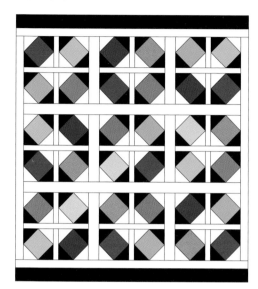

tip BORDER LENGTH

Some fabrics have a width of fabric (WOF) wider than the 40˝ assumed by this pattern. If your fabric has a WOF of at least 42˝, then you do not need to piece your fabric for some of the borders.

First Border

1. Cut 1 bg strip 2˝ × WOF into 4 pieces (about 10˝) and sew each piece to a full bg strip 2˝ × WOF.

2. Trim 2 of the pieced strips to the average height of the quilt, approximately 42˝. Sew the borders onto the sides of the quilt top, pressing the seams open or toward the borders.

3. Trim 2 of the pieced strips to the average width of the quilt, approximately 45˝. Sew the borders onto the top and bottom of the quilt top, pressing the seams open or toward the borders.

Second Border

1. Cut 1 fabric A strip 3″ × WOF in half and sew each piece to a full fabric A strip 3″ × WOF.

2. Trim the pieced strips to the average width of the quilt, approximately 45″. Sew the borders onto the top and bottom of the quilt top, pressing the seams open or toward the borders. The quilt top should measure approximately 45″ × 50″.

Finishing

For complete instructions, refer to Finishing the Quilt (page 121).

1. Make the quilt backing:

■ Remove the selvages. Cut the fabric into 2 pieces (about 53″ × WOF), and sew the backing pieces together along the trimmed selvage edges, using a ½″ seam. Press the seam open. Trim to approximately 53″ × 58″.

or

■ Sew a 14″ × 58″ strip onto a 58″ × WOF piece of fabric to make a 53″ × 58″ backing.

2. Layer the quilt top, batting, and backing. Baste and quilt as desired. *Ships Ahoy* was quilted in a wave design.

3. Bind and enjoy your quilt!

alternate colorway

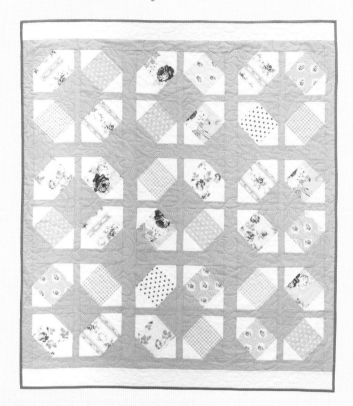

Pieced and quilted by Carol Alperin

FABRICS USED

- **Charm pack:** *Petal Quilting by Tonya Whelan for FreeSpirit Fabrics*
- **Fabric A:** *Bella Solids in White by Moda Fabrics*
- **Background:** *FreeSpirit Solids in Gray by FreeSpirit Fabrics*

Cat's Eye

Pieced and quilted
by Cheryl Brickey

finished quilt

48½˝ × 48½˝

social media

#CatsEyeQuilt

Cat's Eye creates a stunning concentric diamond design using half-square triangles. I used the Woven charm pack for this version of *Cat's Eye* and felt that the gray/white prints were too close to the white background, so I excluded them. This left me with a few charm squares less than the required amount, so I added some solid charm squares from my stash in matching pink and green.

FABRICS USED

- **Charm pack:** *Woven by Bonnie & Camille for Moda Fabrics*
- **Fabric A**: *Bella Solids in Navy by Moda Fabrics*
- **Background:** *Bella Solids in White by Moda Fabrics*

Fabric Requirements

Width of fabric (WOF) is assumed to be at least 40˝.

CHARM SQUARES (5˝ × 5˝): 38

FABRIC A (NAVY): ¾ yard

BACKGROUND (BG) (WHITE): 1⅝ yards

BINDING (STRAIGHT GRAIN): ½ yard

BACKING: 3⅛ yards
or 1⅝ yards with a 18˝ × 57˝ strip pieced on

BATTING: 57˝ × 57˝

Cutting

CHARM SQUARES

- No cutting required; the 38 charm squares will be used as 5˝ × 5˝ squares.

FABRIC A (NAVY)

- Cut 4 strips 5˝ × WOF.

  Subcut the strips into 32 squares 5˝ × 5˝ (each strip can yield 8 squares).

BACKGROUND (BG) (WHITE)

- Cut 9 strips 5˝ × WOF.

  Subcut the strips into 70 squares 5˝ × 5˝ (each strip can yield 8 squares).

- Cut 1 strip 4½˝ × WOF.

  Subcut the strip into 4 squares 4½˝ × 4½˝. These will be used as plain bg blocks.

BINDING

- Cut 5 strips 2½˝ × WOF.

Piecing Units

Use a scant ¼˝ (a thread width smaller than ¼˝) seam throughout the construction of the quilt top unless otherwise instructed.

Half-Square Triangle (HST) Units

1. Place a charm square 5˝ × 5˝ and a bg square 5˝ × 5˝ right sides together. Draw a diagonal line using a removable marking device on the back of the lighter square (shown as the solid line).

2. Sew a ¼˝ seam on both sides of the solid line (shown as the dotted lines). Cut on the solid line and press the seam open or toward the darker fabric.

3. Trim the HST units to 4½˝ × 4½˝. *Each set of 1 charm square and 1 bg square will yield 2 HST units.*

4. Repeat Steps 1–3 to make a total of 76 charm/bg HST units 4½˝ × 4½˝.

5. Repeat Steps 1–3 using fabric A squares 5˝ × 5˝ and bg squares 5˝ × 5˝ to make a total of 64 fabric A/bg HST units 4½˝ × 4½˝.

Quilt Top Assembly

Quadrants

1. Arrange the HST units and pieces in a 6 × 6 arrangement (6 rows of 6 blocks each) as follows.

- 19 charm/bg HST units 4½″ × 4½″
- 16 fabric A/bg HST units 4½″ × 4½″
- 1 bg square 4½″ × 4½″

2. Sew together the HST units and pieces into rows, then sew the rows together, pressing all seams open to make a quadrant 24½″ × 24½″ 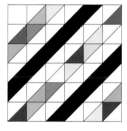 (24″ × 24″ in the finished quilt top).

3. Repeat Steps 1 and 2 to make a total of 4 quadrants.

Piece Quilt Top

1. Arrange the 4 quadrants as shown.

2. Sew together the quadrants into rows, then sew rows together, pressing the seams open. The finished quilt top should measure approximately 48½″ × 48½″.

Finishing

For complete instructions, refer to Finishing the Quilt (page 121).

1. Make the quilt backing:

- Remove the selvages. Cut the fabric into 2 pieces (about 57″ × WOF), and sew the backing pieces together along the trimmed selvage edges, using a ½″ seam. Press the seam open. Trim to approximately 57″ × 57″.

  or

- Sew a 18″ × 57″ strip onto a 57″ × WOF piece of fabric to make a 57″ × 57″ backing.

2. Layer the quilt top, batting, and backing. Baste and quilt as desired. *Cat's Eye* was quilted in a stipple design.

3. Bind and enjoy your quilt!

alternate colorway

Pieced and quilted by Valorie Kasten

FABRICS USED

- *Orange, cream, gold, and purple fabrics from stash*
- ***Fabric A:*** *Kona Cotton Solids in Stone by Robert Kaufman Fabrics*
- ***Background:*** *Pure Solids in White Linen by Art Gallery Fabrics*

Magic Carpet

Pieced by Cindy Kaiser and quilted by Carol Alperin

finished quilt

36½˝ × 42½˝

social media

#MagicCarpetQuilt

Magic Carpet is a fun quilt design that uses hourglass shapes to highlight the charm prints. It is important for this quilt that both the fabric A and background fabric have good contrast with the charm squares and each other to make the design stand out.

FABRICS USED

- ***Charm pack:*** *Natural Beauty by Amy Butler for FreeSpirit Fabrics*

- ***Fabric A***: *Bella Solids in White by Moda Fabrics*

- ***Background***: *Bella Solids in Black by Moda Fabrics*

Fabric Requirements

Width of fabric (WOF) is assumed to be at least 40˝.

CHARM SQUARES (5˝ × 5˝): 32

FABRIC A (WHITE): ½ yard

BACKGROUND (BG) (BLACK): 1½ yards

BINDING (STRAIGHT GRAIN): ½ yard

BACKING: 2½ yards or 1½ yards with a 6˝ × 51˝ strip pieced on

BATTING: 45˝ × 51˝

Cutting

CHARM SQUARES

- Cut 8 charm squares each into 1 rectangle 2¼˝ × 4˝ and 1 square 2¼˝ × 2¼˝.

- Cut 2 charm squares each into 1 rectangle 2¼˝ × 4˝ and 2 squares 2¼˝ × 2¼˝.

- Trim 2 charm squares to 2¾˝ × 2¾˝.

- The remaining 20 charm squares will be used as 5˝ × 5˝ squares.

FABRIC A (WHITE)

- Cut 3 strips 4˝ × WOF.

  Subcut 2 strips into 18 squares 4˝ × 4˝ (each strip can yield 10 squares).
  Subcut 1 strip into 12 rectangles 4˝ × 2¼˝.

BACKGROUND (BG) (BLACK)

- Cut 3 strips 5˝ × WOF.

  Subcut the strips into 20 squares 5˝ × 5˝ (each strip can yield 8 squares).

- Cut 3 strips 4½˝ × WOF for border.

- Cut 3 strips 4˝ × WOF.

  Subcut 2 strips into 20 squares 4˝ × 4˝ (each strip can yield 10 squares).
  Subcut 1 strip into 14 rectangles 4˝ × 2¼˝.

- Cut 1 strip 2¾˝ × WOF.

  Subcut the strip into 2 squares 2¾˝ × 2¾˝ and 14 squares 2¼˝ × 2¼˝.

- Cut 1 strip 2¼˝ × WOF.

  Subcut the strip into 6 additional squares 2¼˝ × 2¼˝.

BINDING

- Cut 5 strips 2½˝ × WOF.

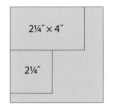

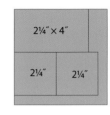

Piecing Units and Blocks

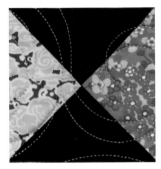

Use a scant ¼″ (a thread width smaller than ¼″) seam throughout the construction of the quilt top unless otherwise instructed.

Half-Square Triangle (HST) Units

1. Place a charm fabric square 2¾″ × 2¾″ and a bg fabric square 2¾″ × 2¾″ right sides together. Draw a diagonal line using a removable marking device on the back of the lighter square (shown as the solid line).

2. Sew a ¼″ seam on both sides of the solid line (shown as the dotted lines). Cut on the solid line and press the seam toward the darker fabric. *Each set of 1 charm and 1 bg fabric square yields 2 HST units.*

3. Trim each HST unit to 2¼″ × 2¼″.

4. Repeat Steps 1–3 to make a total of 4 HST units 2¼″ × 2¼″.

Hourglass Units

1. Place a charm square 5″ × 5″ and a bg fabric square 5″ × 5″ right sides together. Draw a diagonal line using a removable marking device on the back of the lighter square (shown as the solid line).

2. Sew a ¼″ seam on both sides of the solid line (shown as the dotted lines). Cut on the solid line and press the seam toward the darker fabric. *Do not trim these HST units.*

3. Place 2 HST units about 4½″ × 4½″ made with different charm prints right sides together such that the seams nest together and HST units are oriented as shown in the illustration.

4. Draw a diagonal line using a removable marking device on the back of the one of the HST units (shown as the solid line) perpendicular to the seam of that HST unit.

5. Sew a ¼″ seam on each side of the solid line (shown as the dotted lines). Cut on the solid line and press the seams open. Trim hourglass units to 4″ × 4″.

6. Repeat Steps 1–5 to make a total of 40 hourglass units 4″ × 4″ (only 39 are used in the quilt top).

Flying Geese Units

1. Place a bg fabric square 2¼″ × 2¼″ on one side of a charm fabric rectangle 2¼″ × 4″ right sides together.

Draw a diagonal line on the back of the bg fabric square using a removable marking device and sew on the marked line (shown as the dotted line).

Trim a ¼″ from the stitched line and press the seam toward the bg fabric.

2. Place a second bg fabric square 2¼″ × 2¼″ on the opposite end of the charm fabric rectangle and sew together as in Step 1.

3. Trim Flying Geese unit to 2¼″ × 4″ if necessary, making sure there is ¼″ between the point of the charm fabric triangle and the edge of the unit.

4. Repeat Steps 1–3 to make a total of 10 charm/bg Flying Geese units 2¼″ × 4″.

5. Repeat Steps 1–3 using the following pieces to make a total of 6 bg/charm Flying Geese units 2¼″ × 4″.

- 1 bg rectangle 2¼″ × 4″
- 2 charm fabric squares 2¼″ × 2¼″

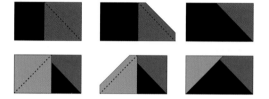

Plain Blocks

The following fabric pieces are used as is (with no further cutting or piecing) as plain blocks in the quilt top.

- 8 bg rectangles 2¼″ × 4″ as bg half-plain blocks
- 12 fabric A rectangles 2¼″ × 4″ as fabric A half-plain blocks
- 20 bg squares 4″ × 4″ as bg full plain blocks
- 18 fabric A squares 4″ × 4″ as fabric A full plain blocks

Quilt Top Assembly

Row A

1. Sew together the following units and blocks, pressing the seams open or toward the plain blocks, to make a row A 2¼″ × 28½″.

- 2 HST units 2¼″ × 2¼″
- 3 bg/charm Flying Geese units 2¼″ × 4″
- 4 bg half-plain blocks 2¼″ × 4″

2. Repeat Step 1 to make a total of 2 row A.

Row B

1. Sew together the following units and blocks, pressing the seams open or toward the plain blocks, to make a row B 4˝ × 28½˝.

- 4 hourglass units 4˝ × 4˝
- 3 fabric A full plain blocks 4˝ × 4˝
- 2 fabric A half-plain blocks 2¼˝ × 4˝

2. Repeat Step 1 to make a total of 6 row B.

Row C

1. Sew together the following units and blocks, pressing the seams open or toward the plain blocks, to make a row C 4˝ × 28½˝.

- 3 hourglass units 4˝ × 4˝
- 2 charm/bg Flying Geese units 2¼˝ × 4˝
- 4 bg full plain blocks 4˝ × 4˝

2. Repeat Step 1 to make a total of 5 row C.

Piece Quilt Top

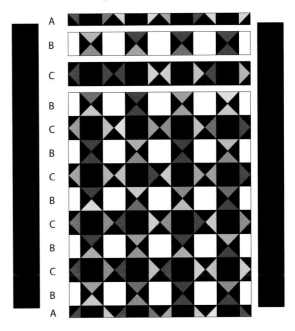

Sew together the following rows, pressing all seams open. The quilt top, before the side borders are added, should measure 28½˝ × 42½˝.

- 2 row A 2¼˝ × 28½˝
- 6 row B 4˝ × 28½˝
- 5 row C 4˝ × 28½˝

Border

tip BORDER LENGTH

Some fabrics have a width of fabric (WOF) wider than the 40˝ assumed by this pattern. If your fabric has a WOF of at least 42½˝, then you do not need to piece your fabric for the borders.

Cut a bg strip 4½˝ × WOF in half, sew each half bg strip to a full bg strip 4½˝ × WOF, and trim to the average height of the quilt top, approximately 42½˝. Sew the borders onto the sides of the quilt, pressing the seams open or toward the borders. The quilt top should measure approximately 36½˝ × 42½˝.

Finishing

For complete instructions, refer to Finishing the Quilt (page 121).

1. Make the quilt backing:

- Remove the selvages. Cut the fabric into 2 pieces (about 45″ × WOF), and sew the backing pieces together along the trimmed selvage edges, using a ½″ seam. Press the seam open. Trim to approximately 45″ × 51″.

or

- Sew a 6″ × 51″ strip onto a 51″ × WOF piece of fabric to make a 45″ × 51″ backing.

2. Layer the quilt top, batting, and backing. Baste and quilt as desired. *Magic Carpet* was quilted in a combination wavy line and bubble design.

3. Bind and enjoy your quilt!

alternate colorway

Pieced by Cheryl Brickey and quilted by Carol Alperin

FABRICS USED

- *Prints cut from my stash with the color inspiration coming from the Half-Square Triangle print from Waterfront Park by Violet Craft for Michael Miller Fabrics*
- **Fabric A:** *Bella Solids in White by Moda Fabrics*
- **Background:** *Bella Solids in Navy by Moda Fabrics*

Circus Stars

Pieced by Cheryl Brickey and
quilted by Carol Alperin

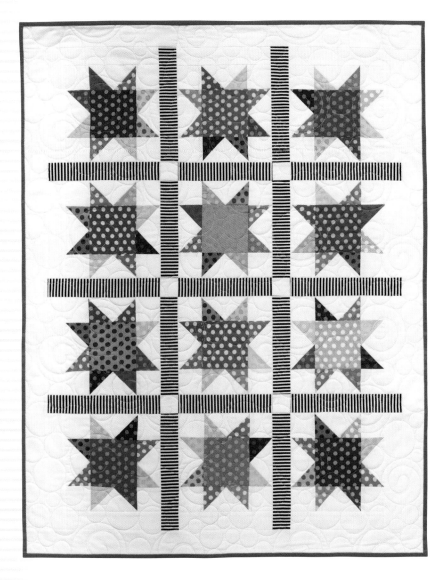

finished block

8″ × 8″

finished quilt

34½″ × 44″

social media

#CircusStarsQuilt

I fell in love with the bright colored polka dot fabrics of this Spot Candy charm pack.
The black-and-white striped fabric paired well with all the bright colors and set off
the stars nicely.

Fabric Requirements

Width of fabric (WOF) is assumed to be at least 40˝.

CHARM SQUARES (5˝ × 5˝): 36

FABRIC A (STRIPED FABRIC):
⅜ yard

BACKGROUND (BG) (WHITE):
1¼ yards

BINDING (STRAIGHT GRAIN):
½ yard

BACKING: 1½ yards

BATTING: 43˝ × 52˝

Cutting

CHARM SQUARES

- Trim 12 charm squares to 4½˝ × 4½˝.

- Cut the remaining 24 charm squares into 4 squares 2½˝ × 2½˝ each for a total of 96 squares.

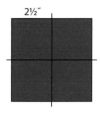

2½˝

FABRIC A (STRIPED FABRIC)

- Cut 5 strips 2˝ × WOF.

  Subcut 3 strips into 10 rectangles 2˝ × 10˝ (each strip can yield 4 rectangles).

  Subcut 2 strips into 7 rectangles 2˝ × 8½˝ (each strip can yield 4 rectangles).

BACKGROUND (BG) (WHITE)

- Cut 13 strips 2½˝ × WOF.

  Subcut 6 strips into 48 rectangles 2½˝ × 4½˝ (each strip can yield 8 rectangles).

  Subcut 3 strips into 48 squares 2½˝ × 2½˝ (each strip can yield 16 squares).

  Reserve 4 strips for border.

- Cut 4 strips 2˝ × WOF.

  Subcut 1 strip into 4 rectangles 2˝ × 10˝.

  Subcut 3 strips into 10 rectangles 2˝ × 8½˝ (each strip can yield 4 rectangles). From the remainder from the strips, cut 6 squares 2˝ × 2˝.

BINDING

- Cut 5 strips 2½˝ × WOF.

FABRICS USED

- **Charm pack:** *Kaffe Classics Spot Candy by Kaffe Fassett for FreeSpirit Fabrics*
- **Fabric A**: *Little Stripe by Michael Miller Fabrics*
- **Background:** *Bella Solids in White by Moda Fabrics*

Piecing the Unit and Block

Use a scant ¼˝ (a thread width smaller than ¼˝) seam throughout the construction of the quilt top unless otherwise instructed.

Flying Geese Units

1. Place a charm fabric square 2½˝ × 2½˝ on one side of a bg rectangle 2½˝ × 4½˝ right sides together.

Draw a diagonal line on the back of the charm fabric square using a removable marking device and sew on the marked line (shown as the dotted line).

Trim a ¼˝ from the stitched line and press the seam toward the bg fabric.

2. Place a charm fabric square 2½˝ × 2½˝ (with a different print) on the opposite end of the bg rectangle and sew together as in Step 1.

3. Trim Flying Geese unit to 2½˝ × 4½˝ if necessary, making sure there is ¼˝ between the point of bg triangle and the edge of the unit.

4. Repeat Steps 1–3 to make a total of 48 Flying Geese units 2½˝ × 4½˝.

Star Blocks

1. Arrange the following units and pieces according to the diagram:

- 1 charm fabric square 4½˝ × 4½˝
- 4 Flying Geese units 2½˝ × 4½˝
- 4 bg squares 2½˝ × 2½˝

2. Sew the units and pieces into rows, pressing the seams open or away from the Flying Geese units. Sew the rows together, pressing the seams open, to make a star block 8½˝ × 8½˝ (8˝ × 8˝ in the finished quilt top).

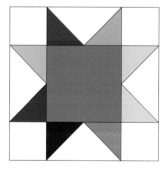

3. Repeat Steps 1 and 2 to make a total of 12 star blocks.

Quilt Top Assembly

Row A

1. Sew a bg rectangle 2″ × 8½″ onto the bottom of a star block to make a unit 8½″ × 10″, pressing the seam open or toward the rectangle.

2. Repeat Step 1 to make a total of 6 units.

3. Sew together the following units and pieces, pressing the seams open or toward the rectangles, to make a row A 10″ × 30½″.

- 3 units (from Step 1) 8½″ × 10″
- 2 bg rectangles 2″ × 10″
- 2 fabric A rectangles 2″ × 10″

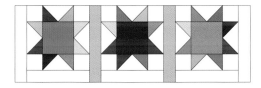

4. Repeat Step 3 to make a total of 2 row A.

Row B

1. Sew together the following blocks and pieces, pressing the seams open or toward the rectangles, to make a row B 8½″ × 30½″.

- 3 star blocks 8½″ × 8½″
- 2 bg rectangles 2″ × 8½″
- 2 fabric A rectangles 2″ × 8½″

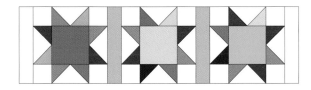

2. Repeat Step 1 to make a total of 2 row B.

Sashing Rows

1. Sew together the following pieces, pressing the seams open or toward the squares, to make a sashing row 2″ × 30½″.

- 2 fabric A rectangles 2″ × 10″
- 1 fabric A rectangle 2″ × 8½″
- 2 bg squares 2″ × 2″

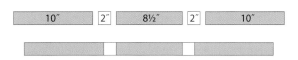

2. Repeat Step 1 to make a total of 3 sashing rows.

Piece Quilt Top

Sew together the following rows as shown, pressing the seams open. The quilt top, before borders are added, should measure 30½″ × 40″.

- 2 row A 10″ × 30½″
- 2 row B 8½″ × 30½″
- 3 sashing rows 2″ × 30½″

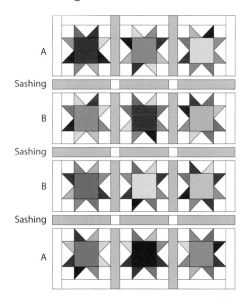

Border

1. Trim 2 strips 2½˝ × WOF to the average height of the quilt, approximately 40˝. Sew the side borders onto the quilt top, pressing the seams open or toward the borders.

2. Trim 2 strips 2½˝ × WOF to the average width of the quilt, approximately 34½˝. Sew the borders onto the top and bottom of the quilt top, pressing the seams open or toward the borders.

The finished quilt top should measure approximately 34½˝ × 44˝.

Finishing

For complete instructions, refer to Finishing the Quilt (page 121).

1. A single width of fabric can be used as the backing.

2. Layer the quilt top, batting, and backing. Baste and quilt as desired. *Circus Stars* was quilted in an allover bubble design.

3. Bind and enjoy your quilt!

alternate colorway

Pieced and quilted by Michele Blake

FABRICS USED

- **Charm pack:** *Clementine by Melody Miller from Ruby Star Society for Moda Fabrics*
- **Fabric A:** *Bella Solids in Baby Pink by Moda Fabrics*
- **Background:** *Bella Solids in White by Moda Fabrics*

Cozy Cottages

Pieced by Cheryl Brickey and quilted by Carol Alperin

finished block
4˝ × 6˝

finished quilt
36½˝ × 44˝

social media
#CozyCottagesQuilt

These houses in *Cozy Cottages* are so charming, perfect for any home or recipient. If you are pressed for time, omit the chimneys from the blocks and make the Flying Geese with two background squares 2½˝ × 2½˝.

Fabric Requirements

Width of fabric (WOF) is assumed to be at least 40˝.

CHARM SQUARES (5˝ × 5˝): 38

FABRIC A (BROWN): ⅛ yard

BACKGROUND (BG) (PINK): 1½ yards

BINDING: ½ yard

BACKING: 2½ yards or 1½ yards with a 6˝ × 52˝ strip pieced on

BATTING: 45˝ × 52˝

Cutting

CHARM SQUARES

- Cut 13 charm squares each into 2 rectangles 2½˝ × 4½˝.

- Trim 25 charm squares to 4½˝ × 4½˝.

FABRIC A (BROWN)

- Cut 2 strips 1˝ × WOF for chimney units.

BACKGROUND (BG) (PINK)

- Cut 4 strips 3½˝ × WOF for border.

- Cut 4 strips 3˝ × WOF for sashing.

- Cut 2 strips 2½˝ × WOF. Subcut the strips into 25 squares 2½˝ × 2½˝ (each strip can yield 16 squares).

- Cut 4 strips 2˝ × WOF. Subcut the strips into 25 rectangles 2˝ × 4½˝ (each strip can yield 8 rectangles).

- Cut 2 strips 1½˝ × WOF for chimney units.

- Cut 2 strips 1˝ × WOF for chimney units.

BINDING

- Cut 5 strips 2½˝ × WOF.

Piecing the Units and Block

Use a scant ¼˝ (a thread width smaller than ¼˝) seam throughout the construction of the quilt top unless otherwise instructed.

FABRICS USED

- **Charm pack:** *Olive's Flower Market by Lella Boutique for Moda Fabrics*
- **Fabric A**: *Bella Solids in Brown by Moda Fabrics*
- **Background:** *Bella Solids in Sisters Pink by Moda Fabrics*

Chimney Units

tip PRESSING FOR SUCCESSFUL STRIP PIECING

I like to press my seams open in strip sets as I find this keeps the seams straighter. This is especially important and helpful when sewing thin strips together like in the chimney units.

1. Sew together the following strips along their long sides to make a strip set. Press the seams open or toward the darker fabric.

- 1 bg strip 1½˝ × WOF
- 1 fabric A strip 1˝ × WOF
- 1 bg strip 1˝ × WOF

2. Repeat Step 1 to make a total of 2 strip sets.

3. Cut the strip sets into 25 chimney units 2½˝ × 2½˝ (each strip can yield 16 chimney units).

Flying Geese Units

1. Place a chimney unit 2½˝ × 2½˝ on one side of a charm fabric rectangle 2½˝ × 4½˝ right sides together.

Be sure that the chimney matches the orientation shown so the chimney is in the correct position in the finished Flying Geese unit.

Draw a diagonal line on the back of the chimney unit using a removable marking device and sew on the marked line (shown as the dotted line).

Trim a ¼˝ from the stitched line and press the seam toward the chimney unit.

2. Place a bg square 2½˝ × 2½˝ on the opposite end of the charm fabric rectangle and sew together as in Step 1.

3. Trim the Flying Geese unit to 2½˝ × 4½˝ if necessary, making sure there is ¼˝ between the point of the charm fabric triangle and the edge of the Flying Geese unit.

4. Repeat Steps 1–3 to make a total of 25 Flying Geese units 2½˝ × 4½˝.

Cottage Blocks

1. Sew together 1 Flying Geese unit 2½″ × 4½″ and 1 charm fabric square 4½″ × 4½″, pressing the seam open or toward the charm fabric square, to make a cottage block 4½″ × 6½″ (4″ × 6″ in the finished quilt top).

2. Repeat Step 1 to make a total of 25 cottage blocks.

Piece Quilt Top Assembly

Column A

1. Sew together the following units and pieces, beginning with a bg rectangle. Press the seams open or toward the bg fabric to make a column A 4½″ × 38″.

- 5 cottage blocks 4½″ × 6½″
- 5 bg rectangles 2″ × 4½″

2. Repeat Step 1 to make a total of 3 column A.

Column B

1. Sew together the following units and pieces, beginning with a cottage block. Press the seams open or toward the bg fabric to make a column B 4½″ × 38″.

- 5 cottage blocks 4½″ × 6½″
- 5 bg rectangles 2″ × 4½″

2. Repeat Step 1 to make a total of 2 column B.

Sashing Strips

Trim the 4 bg strips 3″ × WOF each to 3″ × 38″ to make a total of 4 sashing strips.

Piece Quilt Top

Arrange and sew together the following columns and strips as shown, pressing the seams open or toward the sashing strips. The quilt top, before borders are added, should measure 30½″ × 38″.

- 3 column A 4½″ × 38″
- 2 column B 4½″ × 38″
- 4 sashing strips 3″ × 38″

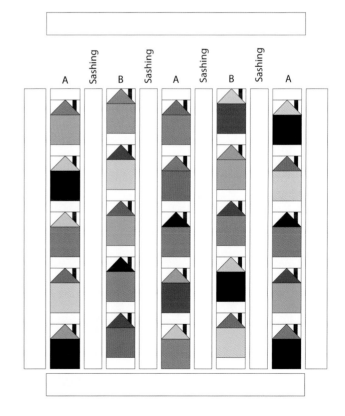

Border

1. Trim 2 strips 3½″ × WOF to the average height of the quilt top, approximately 38″. Sew the side borders onto the sides of the quilt, pressing the seams open or toward the borders.

2. Trim 2 strips 3½″ × WOF to the average width of the quilt top, approximately 36½″. Sew the side borders onto the top and bottom of the quilt, pressing the seams open or toward the borders. The finished quilt top should measure approximately 36½″ × 44″.

Finishing

For complete instructions, refer to Finishing the Quilt (page 121).

1. Make the quilt backing:

- Remove the selvages. Cut the fabric into 2 pieces (about 45″ × WOF), and sew the backing pieces together along the trimmed selvage edges, using a ½″ seam. Press the seam open. Trim to approximately 45″ × 52″.

  or

- Sew a 6″ × 52″ strip onto a 52″ × WOF piece of fabric to make a 45″ × 52″ backing.

2. Layer the quilt top, batting, and backing. Baste and quilt as desired. *Cozy Cottages* was quilted in a cloud like design.

3. Bind and enjoy your quilt!

alternate colorway

Pieced by Sarah Snider and quilted by Carol Alperin

FABRICS USED

- **Charm pack:** *Breeze by Zen Chic for Moda Fabrics*
- **Fabric A:** *Bella Solids in Brown by Moda Fabrics*
- **Background:** *Breeze White and Coral Pluses by Zen Chic for Moda Fabrics*

Ninja

Pieced by Cheryl Brickey and quilted by Carol Alperin

finished block

12″ × 12″

finished quilt

42½″ × 47½″

social media

#NinjaQuilt

Ninja earned its name from the ninja-like star blocks featured in the pattern. I used a fat quarter bundle, and I cut two charm squares from each fat quarter (excluding a few that I felt were too close to the white fabric A). I was even able to use some of the leftover fat quarters for the backing.

Fabric Requirements

Width of fabric (WOF) is assumed to be at least 40˝.

CHARM SQUARES (5˝ × 5˝): 29

FABRIC A (WHITE): ⅝ yard

BACKGROUND (BG) (BLUE): 1⅜ yards

BINDING (STRAIGHT GRAIN): ½ yard

BACKING: 2⅞ yards or 1⅝ yards with a 12˝ × 56˝ strip pieced on

BATTING: 51˝ × 56˝

Cutting

CHARM SQUARES

- Cut 11 charm squares in half to make 22 rectangles 2½˝ × 5˝.

- The remaining 18 charm squares will be used as 5˝ × 5˝ squares.

FABRIC A (WHITE)

- Cut 2 strips 4½˝ × WOF.

  Subcut the strips into 9 squares 4½˝ × 4½˝ (each strip can yield 8 squares).

- Cut 3 strips 2½˝ × WOF.

  Subcut the strips into 20 rectangles 2½˝ × 5˝ (each strip can yield 8 squares).

BACKGROUND (BG) (BLUE)

- Cut 3 strips 5˝ × WOF.

  Subcut 2 strips into 16 squares 5˝ × 5˝ (each strip can yield 8 squares).

  Subcut 1 strip into 2 squares 5˝ × 5˝ and 4 squares 4½˝ × 4½˝.

- Cut 5 strips 4½˝ × WOF.

  Subcut 1 strip into 3 rectangles 4½˝ × 12½˝.

  Subcut 4 strips into 32 additional squares 4½˝ × 4½˝ (each strip can yield 8 squares).

- Cut 5 strips 1½˝ × WOF for first border.

BINDING

- Cut 5 strips 2½˝ × WOF.

FABRICS USED

- **Charm pack:** *Flower Shop by Patty Sloniger for Michael Miller Fabrics*

- **Fabric A**: *Bella solids in White by Moda Fabrics*

- **Background**: *Bella solids in Frost by Moda Fabrics*

Piecing the Unit and Blocks

Use a scant ¼˝ (a thread width smaller than ¼˝) seam throughout the construction of the quilt top unless otherwise instructed.

Half-Square Triangle (HST) Units

1. Place a charm square 5˝ × 5˝ and a bg square 5˝ × 5˝ right sides together. Draw a diagonal line using a removable marking device on the back of the lighter square (shown as the solid line).

2. Sew a ¼˝ seam on both sides of the solid line (shown as the dotted lines). Cut on the solid line and press the seam open or toward the darker fabric.

3. Trim the HST units to 4½˝ × 4½˝. *Each set of 1 charm square and 1 fabric A square yields 2 HST units.*

4. Repeat Steps 1–3 to make a total of 36 HST units 4½˝ × 4½˝.

Left-Twisting Blocks

1. Arrange the following units and pieces as shown, making sure that the orientation of the pieces matches the illustration:

- 4 HST units 4½˝ × 4½˝
- 4 bg squares 4½˝ × 4½˝
- 1 fabric A square 4½˝ × 4½˝

2. Sew the units and pieces into rows, pressing the seams open or away from the HST units. Sew the rows together, pressing the seams open, to make a left-twisting block 12½˝ × 12½˝.

3. Repeat Steps 1 and 2 to make a total of 6 left-twisting blocks 12½˝ × 12½˝ (12˝ × 12˝ finished in the quilt top).

Right-Twisting Blocks

1. Arrange the following units and pieces as shown, making sure that the orientation of the pieces matches the illustration:

- 4 HST units 4½˝ × 4½˝
- 4 bg squares 4½˝ × 4½˝
- 1 fabric A square 4½˝ × 4½˝

2. Sew the units and pieces into rows, pressing the seams open or away from the HST units. Sew the rows together, pressing the seams open, to make a right-twisting block 12½˝ × 12½˝.

3. Repeat Steps 1 and 2 to make a total of 3 right-twisting blocks 12½˝ × 12½˝ (12˝ × 12˝ finished in the quilt top).

Quilt Top Assembly

Left Row

1. Sew together 3 left-twisting blocks and a bg rectangle 4½˝ × 12½˝, pressing the seams open, to make a left row 12½˝ × 40½˝.

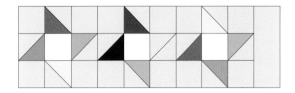

2. Repeat Step 1 to make a total of 2 left rows.

Right Row

Sew together 3 right-twisting blocks and a bg rectangle 4½˝ × 12½˝, pressing the seams open, to make a right row 12½˝ × 40½˝.

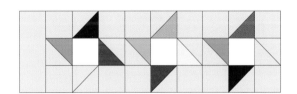

Piece Quilt Top

Sew together the 2 left rows and 1 right row as shown in the quilt top assembly diagram (at right), pressing the seams open. The quilt top, before adding borders, should measure approximately 40½˝ × 36½˝.

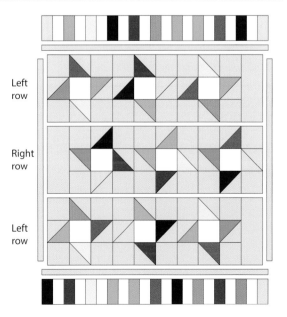

Left row

Right row

Left row

First Border

1. Trim 2 of the bg fabric strips 1½˝ × WOF to the average height of the quilt, approximately 36½˝, and sew onto the sides of the quilt, pressing the seams open or toward the borders.

tip BORDER LENGTH

Some fabrics have a width of fabric (WOF) wider than the 40˝ assumed by this pattern. If your fabric has a WOF of at least 42½˝, then you do not need to piece your fabric for the borders in Step 2.

2. Cut 1 bg fabric strip 1½˝ × WOF in half, sew each half-strip to a full blue fabric strip 1½˝ × WOF, and trim to the average width of the quilt, approximately 42½˝. Sew the borders onto the top and bottom of the quilt top, pressing the seams open or toward the borders. The quilt top, after the first border is added, should measure 42½˝ × 38½˝.

Piano Key Border

1. Sew together 11 charm fabric rectangles 2½˝ × 5˝ alternating with 10 fabric A rectangles 2½˝ × 5˝ (starting and ending with the charm fabric rectangles) to make the piano key border 5˝ × 42½˝.

2. Repeat Step 1 to make a total of 2 piano key borders.

3. Sew the piano key borders onto the top and bottom of the quilt top. The finished quilt top should measure approximately 42½˝ × 47½˝.

Finishing

For complete instructions, refer to Finishing the Quilt (page 121).

1. Make the quilt backing:

- Remove the selvages. Cut the fabric into 2 pieces (about 51˝ × WOF) and sew the backing pieces together along the trimmed selvage edges, using a ½˝ seam. Press the seam open. Trim to approximately 51˝ × 56˝.

or

- Sew a 12˝ × 56˝ strip onto a 56˝ × WOF piece of fabric to make a 51˝ × 56˝ backing.

2. Layer the quilt top, batting, and backing. Baste and quilt as desired. *Ninja* was quilted in a swirl design.

3. Bind and enjoy your quilt!

alternate colorway

Pieced and quilted by Cindy Lammon

FABRICS USED

- **Charm pack:** *Darlings by Ruby Star Society for Moda Fabrics*
- **Fabric A:** *Bella Solids in White by Moda Fabrics*
- **Background:** *FreeSpirit Solids in Gray by FreeSpirit Fabrics*

Bowtie

Pieced by Cheryl Brickey and quilted by Carol Alperin

finished block

8″ × 8″

finished quilt

40½″ × 48½″

social media

#BowtieQuilt

Bowtie combines a bow tie–like design with an Irish chain diagonal row for a great smaller quilt.

Fabric Requirements

Width of fabric (WOF) is assumed to be at least 40˝.

CHARM SQUARES (5˝ × 5˝): 30

FABRIC A (GRAY): ⅜ yard

BACKGROUND (BG) (WHITE): 1½ yards

BINDING (STRAIGHT GRAIN): ½ yard

BACKING: 2¾ yards
or 1⅝ yards with a
10˝ × 57˝ strip pieced on

BATTING: 49˝ × 57˝

Cutting

CHARM SQUARES

- No cutting required;
  the 30 charm squares
  will be used as 5˝ × 5˝ squares.

FABRIC A (GRAY)

- Cut 4 strips 2½˝ × WOF for Irish units.

BACKGROUND (BG) (WHITE)

- Cut 4 strips 5˝ × WOF.

  Subcut the strips into 30 squares
  5˝ × 5˝ (each strip can yield
  8 squares).

- Cut 4 strips 4½˝ × WOF.

  Subcut the strips into 30 squares
  4½˝ × 4½˝ (each strip can yield
  8 squares).

- Cut 4 strips 2½˝ × WOF for Irish units.

BINDING

- Cut 5 strips 2½˝ × WOF.

Piecing the Units and Blocks

Use a scant ¼˝ (a thread width smaller than ¼˝) seam throughout the construction of the quilt top unless otherwise instructed.

Irish Units

1. Sew together 1 fabric A strip 2½˝ × WOF and 1 bg strip 2½˝ × WOF along their long sides to make a strip set. Press the seams open or toward the darker fabric.

2. Repeat Step 1 to make a total of 4 strip sets.

3. Cut the strip sets into 60 units 2½˝ × 4½˝ (each strip can yield 16 units).

4. Sew together 2 units from Step 2, as shown. Press the seam open to make an Irish unit 4½˝ × 4½˝.

5. Repeat Step 4 to make a total of 30 Irish units.

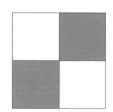

Half-Square Triangle (HST) Units

1. Place a charm square 5˝ × 5˝ and a bg square 5˝ × 5˝ right sides together. Draw a diagonal line using a removable marking device on the back of the lighter square (shown as the solid line).

2. Sew a ¼″ seam on both sides of the solid line (shown as the dotted lines). Cut on the solid line and press the seam open or toward the darker fabric.

3. Trim the HST units to 4½″ × 4½″. *Each set of 1 charm square and 1 bg square yields 2 HST units.*

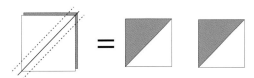

4. Repeat Steps 1–3 to make a total of 60 HST units 4½″ × 4½″.

Block Assembly

1. Arrange the following pieces, making sure that the orientation of the pieces matches the illustration.

- 2 HST units 4½″ × 4½″
- 1 Irish unit 4½″ × 4½″
- 1 bg square 4½″ × 4½″

2. Sew the pieces into rows, pressing the seams open or away from the HST units. Sew the rows together, pressing the seams open, to make a block 8½″ × 8½″ 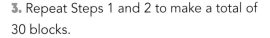 (8″ × 8″ in the finished quilt top).

3. Repeat Steps 1 and 2 to make a total of 30 blocks.

Quilt Top Assembly

1. Arrange the blocks in a 5 × 6 arrangement (6 rows of 5 blocks each), rotating the blocks as shown.

2. Sew the blocks into rows, pressing the seams open. Sew together the rows, pressing the seams open to make the quilt top. The quilt top should measure approximately 40½″ × 48½″.

Finishing

For complete instructions, refer to Finishing the Quilt (page 121).

1. Make the quilt backing:

- Remove the selvages. Cut the fabric into 2 pieces (about 49″ × WOF), and sew the backing pieces together along the trimmed selvage edges, using a ½″ seam. Press the seam open. Trim to approximately 49″ × 57″.

  or

- Sew a 10″ × 57″ strip onto a 57″ × WOF piece of fabric to make a 49″ × 57″ backing.

2. Layer the quilt top, batting, and backing. Baste and quilt as desired. *Bowtie* was quilted in a floral design.

3. Bind and enjoy your quilt!

alternate colorway

Pieced and quilted by Cindy Hocker Lange

FABRICS USED

- **Charm pack:** *Bonnie and Camille prints from stash*
- **Fabric A:** *Bella Solids in Navy by Moda Fabrics*
- **Background:** *Bella Solids in White by Moda Fabrics*

Nine-Patch Challenge

Pieced and quilted by Cheryl Brickey

finished block

6″ × 6″

finished quilt

46″ × 54½″

social media

#NinePatchChallengeQuilt

The Nine-Patch blocks in this quilt are turned on point which gives this quilt the look of granny squares. Chicopee has always been one of my favorite fabric lines and I was excited to see it paired with this gray linen looking background fabric.

FABRICS USED

• **Charm pack:** *Chicopee by Denyse Schimdt for FreeSpirit Fabrics*

• **Fabric A**: *Bella Solids in White by Moda Fabrics*

• **Background:** *Dublin in Linen by Deborah Edwards for Northcott Fabrics*

Fabric Requirements

Width of fabric (WOF) is assumed to be at least 40˝.

CHARM SQUARES (5˝ × 5˝): 38

FABRIC A (WHITE): ¾ yard

BACKGROUND (BG) (GRAY): 1¾ yards

BINDING (STRAIGHT GRAIN): ½ yard

BACKING: 3 yards or 1¾ yards with a 15˝ × 63˝ strip pieced on

BATTING: 54˝ × 63˝

Cutting

CHARM SQUARES

■ Cut each charm square into 4 squares 2½˝ × 2½˝.

For 30 charm squares, keep the cut 2½˝ × 2½˝ squares together in matching sets of 4 (these are used together in one block).

The remaining 2½˝ × 2½˝ squares are used as the center print square in the blocks (there will be 2 extra squares not used in the quilt top).

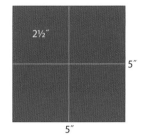

FABRIC A (WHITE)

■ Cut 8 strips 2½˝ × WOF.

Subcut the strips into 120 squares 2½˝ × 2½˝ (each strip can yield 16 squares).

BACKGROUND (BG) (GRAY)

tip OVERSIZING SETTING TRIANGLES

If you like to oversize your setting triangles (for a little wiggle room during quilt top assembly), then cut the squares to 10¼˝ × 10¼˝ instead of 9¾˝ × 9¾˝ and 5½˝ × 5½˝ instead of 5⅛˝ × 5⅛˝.

■ Cut 2 strips 9¾˝ × WOF.

Subcut 1 strip into 4 squares 9¾˝ × 9¾˝.

Subcut 1 strip into 1 square 9¾˝ × 9¾˝ and 2 squares 5⅛˝ × 5⅛˝.

■ Cut 4 strips 6½˝ × WOF.

Subcut the strips into 20 squares 6½˝ × 6½˝ (each strip can yield 6 squares).

■ Cut 6 strips 2˝ × WOF for border.

BINDING

■ Cut 6 strips 2½˝ × WOF.

Piecing the Blocks

Use a scant ¼˝ (a thread width smaller than ¼˝) seam throughout the construction of the quilt top unless otherwise instructed.

Nine-Patch Blocks

1. Arrange the following pieces as shown. Sew the pieces into rows, pressing away from the fabric A squares. Sew the rows together, pressing the seams open, to make a Nine-Patch block 6½˝ × 6½˝ (6˝ × 6˝ in the finished quilt top).

- 4 matching charm fabric squares 2½˝ × 2½˝
- 1 additional charm fabric square 2½˝ × 2½˝
- 4 fabric A squares 2½˝ × 2½˝

2. Repeat Step 1 to make a total of 30 Nine-Patch blocks.

Setting Triangles

1. Cut the 5 squares 9¾˝ × 9¾˝ in half twice on the diagonals to make 20 side-setting triangles (you will have 2 extra side-setting triangles).

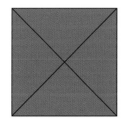

2. Cut the 2 squares 5⅛˝ × 5⅛˝ in half once on the diagonal to make the corner setting triangles.

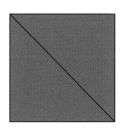

Quilt Top Assembly

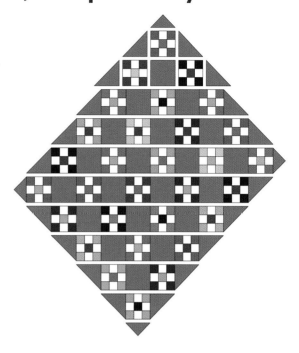

1. Arrange the Nine-Patch blocks, plain bg blocks, side-setting triangles, and corner triangles listed and shown for an on-point setting quilt top.

- 30 Nine-Patch blocks 6½˝ × 6½˝
- 20 bg blocks 6½˝ × 6½˝
- 18 side-setting triangles
- 4 corner triangles

2. Sew the blocks, side-setting triangles, and corner triangles together into diagonal rows, pressing all seams open.

3. Sew the rows together to form the quilt top, pressing the seams open. The quilt top, before the border is added, should measure approximately 43˝ × 51½˝.

Border

1. Cut 1 bg strip 2″ × WOF in half and sew each half to a full bg strip 2″ × WOF. Trim to the average height of the quilt, approximately 51½″. Sew the side borders onto the quilt top, pressing the seams open or toward the borders.

2. Cut 1 bg strip 2″ × WOF in half and sew each half to a full bg strip 2″ × WOF. Trim to the average width of the quilt, approximately 46″. Sew the borders onto the top and bottom of the quilt top, pressing the seams open or toward the borders. The quilt top should measure approximately 46″ × 54½″.

Finishing

For complete instructions, refer to Finishing the Quilt (page 121).

1. Make the quilt backing:

- Remove the selvages. Cut the fabric into 2 pieces (about 54″ × WOF) and sew the backing pieces together along the trimmed selvage edges, using a ½″ seam. Press the seam open. Trim to approximately 54″ × 63″.

or

- Sew a 15″ × 63″ strip onto a 63″ × WOF piece of fabric to make a 54″ × 63″ backing.

2. Layer the quilt top, batting, and backing. Baste and quilt as desired. *Nine-Patch Challenge* was quilted by echoing the seamlines.

3. Bind and enjoy your quilt!

alternate colorway

Pieced and quilted by Garen Sherwood

FABRICS USED

- **Charm pack:** *Sugarhouse by Amy Smart for Riley Blake Designs*
- **Fabric A:** *Bella Solids in White by Moda Fabrics*
- **Background:** *Kona Cotton Solids in Parchment by Robert Kaufman Fabrics*

One-Eyed Monster

Pieced and quilted
by Cheryl Brickey

finished block

10½˝ × 10½˝

finished quilt

42½˝ × 42½˝

social media

#OneEyedMonsterQuilt

The blocks from *One-Eyed Monster* remind me of little monsters or robots that only have one large eye. The neutral colors of the background and the secondary fabric (the eye of the "monster") make the charm pack colors pop.

Fabric Requirements

Width of fabric (WOF) is assumed to be at least 40˝.

CHARM SQUARES (5˝ × 5˝): 32

FABRIC A (BLACK): ⅛ yard

BACKGROUND (BG) (WHITE): 1¾ yards

BINDING (STRAIGHT GRAIN): ½ yard

BACKING: 2⅞ yards
or 1½ yards with a 12˝ × 51˝ strip pieced on

BATTING: 51˝ × 51˝

Cutting

CHARM SQUARES

- No cutting required; the 32 charm squares will be used as 5˝ × 5˝ squares.

FABRIC A (BLACK)

- Cut 1 strip 2˝ × WOF for center units.

BACKGROUND (BG) (WHITE)

- Cut 4 strips 5˝ × WOF.

  Subcut the strips into 32 squares 5˝ × 5˝ (each strip can yield 8 squares).

- Cut 7 strips 4˝ × WOF.

  Subcut the strips into 64 squares 4˝ × 4˝ (each strip can yield 10 squares).

- Cut 6 strips 1½˝ × WOF.

  Subcut 4 strips into 32 rectangles 1½˝ × 4˝ (each strip can yield 10 rectangles).
  Reserve 2 strips for center units.

BINDING

- Cut 5 strips 2½˝ × WOF.

Piecing the Units and Blocks

Use a scant ¼˝ (a thread width smaller than ¼˝) seam throughout the construction of the quilt top unless otherwise instructed.

Center Units

1. Sew together 2 bg fabric strips 1½˝ × WOF and 1 fabric A strip 2˝ × WOF along their long sides to make a strip set. Press the seams open or toward the darker fabric.

2. Cut the strip set into 16 segments 2˝ × 4˝.

3. Sew together 1 segment 2˝ × 4˝ from Step 2 and 2 bg rectangles 1½˝ × 4˝, pressing the seams open, to make a center unit 4˝ × 4˝.

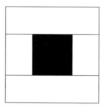

4. Repeat Step 3 to make a total of 16 center units.

Half-Square Triangle (HST) Units

1. Place a charm square 5″ × 5″ and a bg fabric square 5″ × 5″ right sides together. Draw a diagonal line using a removable marking device on the back of the lighter square (shown as the solid line).

2. Sew a ¼″ seam on both sides of the solid line (shown as the dotted lines). Cut on the

solid line and press the seam toward the darker fabric. *Do not trim the HST units.*

3. Repeat Steps 1 and 2 to make a total of 64 HST units about 4½″ × 4½″.

Hourglass Units

1. Select a first set of 2 matching HST units about 4½″ × 4½″ and a second set of 2 matching HST units about 4½″ × 4½″.

2. Place a HST unit from the first set and a HST unit from the second set right sides together such that the seams nest together and HST unit are oriented as shown in the illustration. Repeat with other 2 HST units from the first and second sets. *This will create 4 matching hourglass units.*

3. Draw a diagonal line using a removable marking device on the back of the one of the HST units (shown as the solid line) perpendicular to the seam of that HST unit.

4. Sew a ¼″ seam on each side of the solid line (shown as the dotted lines). Cut on the solid line and press the seams open. Trim the Hourglass blocks to 4″ × 4″.

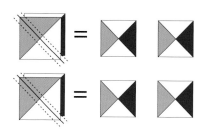

5. Repeat Steps 1–4 to make a total of 64 hourglass units 4″ × 4″ (16 sets of 4 matching hourglass units each).

Blocks

1. Arrange the following units and pieces listed and as shown, making sure that the orientation of the pieces matches the illustration.

- 1 center unit 4″ × 4″
- 4 hourglass units 4″ × 4″
- 4 bg fabric squares 4″ × 4″

2. Sew the units and pieces into rows, pressing the seams open. Sew the rows together, pressing the seams open, to make a block 11″ × 11″

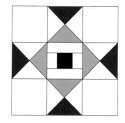

(10½″ × 10½″ finished in the quilt top).

Quilt Top Assembly

1. Arrange the blocks in a 4 × 4 arrangement (4 rows of 4 blocks each) as shown.

2. Sew the blocks into rows, pressing the seams open. Sew the rows together, pressing the seams open to make the quilt top. The quilt top should measure approximately 42½″ × 42½″.

Finishing

For complete instructions, refer to Finishing the Quilt (page 121).

1. Make the quilt backing:

- Remove the selvages. Cut the fabric into 2 pieces (about 51″ × WOF), and sew the backing pieces together along the trimmed selvage edges, using a ½″ seam. Press the seam open. Trim to approximately 51″ × 51″.

or

- Sew a 12″ × 51″ strip onto a 51″ × WOF piece of fabric to make a 51″ × 51″ backing.

2. Layer the quilt top, batting, and backing. Baste and quilt as desired. *One-Eyed Monster* was quilted in an open bear claw design.

3. Bind and enjoy your quilt!

alternate colorway

Pieced and quilted by Delia Dorn

FABRICS USED

- **Charm pack:** *Crescent by Sarah Watts from Ruby Star Society for Moda Fabrics*
- **Fabric A:** *Bella Solids in Tangerine by Moda Fabrics*
- **Background:** *Bella Solids in White by Moda Fabrics*

Baskets

Pieced by Cheryl Brickey and
quilted by Carol Alperin

finished block
20˝ × 20˝

finished quilt
45½˝ × 49½˝

social media
#BasketsQuilt

Baskets comes together easily using half-square triangles and squares pieced
together in four large blocks. In this version, the Basket blocks are oriented in
a circle, but you could change them to all face inward, outward, or in the same
direction for a different look.

Fabric Requirements

Width of fabric (WOF) is assumed to be at least 40˝.

CHARM SQUARES (5˝ × 5˝): 36

FABRIC A (BROWN): ½ yard

BACKGROUND (BG) (WHITE): 1¾ yards

BINDING (STRAIGHT GRAIN): ½ yard

BACKING: 3 yards or 1⅔ yards with a 15˝ × 58˝ strip pieced on

BATTING: 54˝ × 58˝

Cutting

CHARM SQUARES

- Trim 4 charm squares to 4½˝ × 4½˝.

- Cut 10 charm squares in half to make 20 rectangles 2½˝ × 5˝.

- The remaining 22 charm squares will be used as 5˝ × 5˝ squares.

FABRIC A (BROWN)

- Cut 1 strip 5˝ × WOF.

  Subcut the strip into 8 squares 5˝ × 5˝.

- Cut 1 strip 4½˝ × WOF.

  Subcut the strip into 4 squares 4½˝ × 4½˝.

BACKGROUND (BG) (WHITE)

- Cut 4 strips 5˝ × WOF.

  Subcut the strips into 30 squares 5˝ × 5˝ (each strip can yield 8 squares).

- Cut 4 strips 4½˝ × WOF.

  Subcut 3 strips into 8 rectangles 4½˝ × 12½˝ (each strip can yield 3 rectangles).
  Subcut 1 strip into 8 squares 4½˝ × 4½˝.

- Cut 5 strips 3˝ × WOF for first border.

BINDING

- Cut 6 strips 2½˝ × WOF.

Piecing the Units, Sections, and Blocks

Use a scant ¼˝ (a thread width smaller than ¼˝) seam throughout the construction of the quilt top unless otherwise instructed.

Half-Square Triangle (HST) Units

1. Place a charm square 5˝ × 5˝ and a bg square 5˝ × 5˝ right sides together. Draw a diagonal line using a removable marking device on the back of the lighter square (shown as the solid line).

2. Sew a ¼˝ seam on both sides of the solid line (shown as the dotted lines). Cut on the solid line and press the seam open or toward the darker fabric.

3. Trim the HST units to 4½˝ × 4½˝. *Each set of 1 charm or fabric A square and 1 bg square will yield 2 HST units.*

4. Repeat Steps 1–3 to make a total of 44 charm/bg HST units 4½˝ × 4½˝.

5. Repeat Steps 1–3 using fabric A squares 5˝ × 5˝ and bg squares 5˝ × 5˝ to make a total of 16 fabric A/bg HST units 4½˝ × 4½˝.

Top Sections

1. Arrange together the following pieces listed, making sure that the orientation of the pieces matches the illustration.

- 9 charm/bg HST units 4½˝ × 4½˝
- 1 fabric A/bg HST unit 4½˝ × 4½˝
- 1 charm fabric square 4½˝ × 4½˝
- 1 bg square 4½˝ × 4½˝

2. Sew the pieces into rows, pressing the seams open. Sew the rows together, then sew a bg rectangle 4½˝ × 12½˝ on the left side, pressing the seam open, to make a top section 12½˝ × 20½˝.

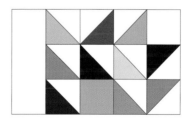

3. Repeat Steps 1 and 2 to make a total of 4 top sections.

Bottom Sections

1. Arrange and sew together the following pieces listed, making sure that the orientation of the pieces matches the illustration.

- 2 charm/bg HST units 4½″ × 4½″
- 3 fabric A/bg HST units 4½″ × 4½″
- 1 fabric A square 4½″ × 4½″
- 1 bg square 4½″ × 4½″
- 1 bg rectangle 4½″ × 12½″

2. Sew the pieces into rows, pressing the seams open. Sew the rows together, pressing the seam open, to make a bottom section 8½″ × 20½″.

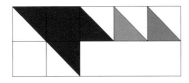

3. Repeat Steps 1 and 2 to make a total of 4 bottom sections.

Block Assembly

1. Sew together 1 top section 12½″ × 20½″ and 1 bottom section 8½″ × 20½″, pressing the seam open, to make a block 20½″ × 20½″ (20″ × 20″ in the finished quilt top).

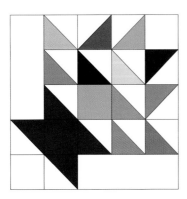

2. Repeat Step 1 to make a total of 4 blocks.

Quilt Top Assembly

1. Arrange the blocks in a 2 × 2 arrangement (2 rows of 2 blocks each), rotating the blocks to match the quilt top assembly diagram.

2. Sew the blocks into rows, then sew the rows together, pressing the seams open, to make the quilt top. The quilt top, before borders are added, should measure approximately 40½″ × 40½″.

Adding Borders

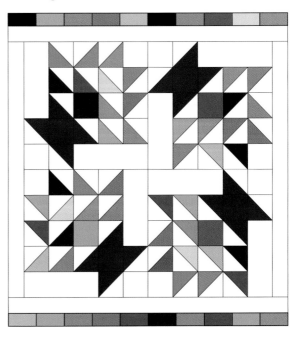

tip BORDER LENGTH

Some fabrics have a width of fabric (WOF) wider than the 40˝ assumed by this pattern. If your fabric has a WOF of at least 40½˝, then you do *not* need to piece your fabric for the side borders (First Border, Step 1).

First Border

1. Cut 1 bg strip 3˝ × WOF into 4 pieces (3˝ × about 10˝) and sew each bg piece 3˝ × about 10˝ to a full bg strip 3˝ × WOF.

2. Trim 2 of the pieced bg strips to the average height of the quilt top, approximately 40½˝ and sew onto the sides of the quilt, pressing the seams open or toward the borders.

3. Trim 2 of the pieced bg strips to the average width of the quilt top, approximately 45½˝ and sew onto the top and bottom of the quilt, pressing the seams open or toward the borders. The quilt top, after the first border is added, should measure 45½˝ × 45½˝.

Second Border

1. Sew together 10 charm fabric rectangles 2½˝ × 5˝, pressing the seams open or toward the darker fabrics, to make a second border 2½˝ × 45½˝.

2. Repeat Step 1 to make a total of 2 second borders.

3. Sew second borders onto the top and bottom of the quilt top, pressing the seams open or toward the second borders. The quilt top should measure approximately 45½˝ × 49½˝.

Finishing

For complete instructions, refer to Finishing the Quilt (page 121).

1. Make the quilt backing:

- Remove the selvages. Cut the fabric into 2 pieces (about 54˝ × WOF), and sew the backing pieces together along the trimmed selvage edges, using a ½˝ seam. Press the seam open. Trim to approximately 54˝ × 58˝.

  or

- Sew a 15˝ × 58˝ strip onto a 58˝ × WOF piece of fabric to make a 54˝ × 58˝ backing.

2. Layer the quilt top, batting, and backing. Baste and quilt as desired. *Baskets* was quilted in a square stipple design.

3. Bind and enjoy your quilt!

alternate colorway

Pieced by Ruth Freyer and quilted by Carol Alperin

FABRICS USED

- **Charm pack:** *Lollipop Garden by Lella Boutique for Moda Fabrics*
- **Fabric A:** *Kona Cotton Solids in Eggplant by Robert Kaufman Fabrics*
- **Background:** *Bella Solids in White by Moda Fabrics*

Coin Flip

Pieced and quilted by Cheryl Brickey

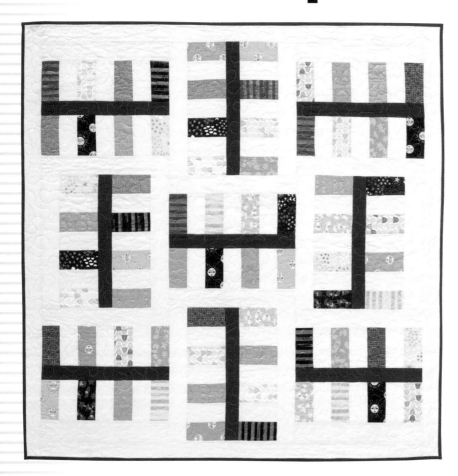

finished block
14″ × 14″

finished quilt
46½″ × 46½″

social media
#CoinFlipQuilt

Coin Flip is a very beginner-friendly design. It is a cross between a coin quilt and piano key design. With only nine blocks, it sews up swiftly and is ready for quilting in no time.

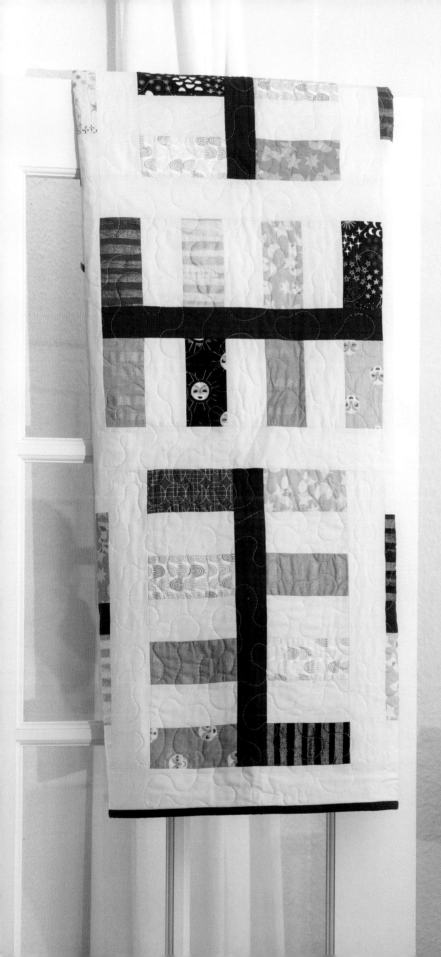

Fabric Requirements

Width of fabric (WOF) is assumed to be at least 40˝.

CHARM SQUARES (5˝ × 5˝): 36

FABRIC A (DARK PURPLE): ⅜ yard

BACKGROUND (BG) (OFF-WHITE): 1⅝ yards

BINDING (STRAIGHT GRAIN): ½ yard

BACKING: 3 yards
or 1⅝ yards with a
16˝ × 55˝ strip pieced on

BATTING: 55˝ × 55˝

Cutting

CHARM SQUARES

- Cut each charm square in half to make 72 charm fabric rectangles 2½˝ × 5˝.

FABRIC A (DARK PURPLE)

- Cut 5 strips 2˝ × WOF.

  Subcut 5 strips into 9 rectangles 2˝ × 14½˝ (each strip can yield 2 rectangles).

BACKGROUND (BG) (OFF-WHITE)

- Cut 12 strips 2½˝ × WOF.

  Subcut 7 strips into 54 rectangles 2½˝ × 5˝ (each strip can yield 8 rectangles). Reserve 5 strips for border.

- Cut 9 strips 2¼˝ × WOF.

  Subcut the strips into 18 rectangles 2¼˝ × 14½˝ (each strip can yield 2 rectangles).

BINDING

- Cut 5 strips 2½˝ × WOF.

Piecing the Units and Blocks

Use a scant ¼˝ (a thread width smaller than ¼˝) seam throughout the construction of the quilt top unless otherwise instructed.

Use a variety of charm prints within the units and blocks.

1. Sew together 4 charm fabric rectangles 2½˝ × 5˝ and 3 bg rectangles 2½˝ × 5˝, pressing the seams open or toward the darker fabric, to make a unit 5˝ × 14½˝.

2. Sew together the following units and pieces, pressing the seams open or toward the darker fabrics, to make a block 14½˝ × 14½˝ (14˝ × 14˝ in the finished quilt top).

- 2 units 5˝ × 14½˝ from Step 1
- 1 fabric A rectangle 2˝ × 14½˝
- 2 bg rectangles 2¼˝ × 14½˝

3. Repeat Steps 1 and 2 to make a total of 9 blocks.

Quilt Top Assembly

1. Arrange the blocks in a 3 × 3 arrangement (3 rows of 3 blocks each) and rotate the blocks so that each block is 90° from its neighboring blocks as shown.

2. Sew the blocks into rows and then sew the rows together, pressing the seams open. The quilt top, before borders are added, should measure 42½˝ × 42½˝.

Border

tip BORDER LENGTH

Some fabrics have a width of fabric (WOF) wider than the 40˝ assumed by this pattern. If your fabric has a WOF of at least 42½˝, then you do not need to piece your fabric for the side borders (Step 2, below).

1. Cut 1 bg strip 2½˝ × WOF into 4 pieces (about 2½˝ × 10˝) and sew each bg piece 2½˝ × 10˝ to a full bg strip 2½˝ × WOF.

2. Trim 2 of the pieced bg strips to the average height of the quilt top, approximately 42½˝ and sew onto the sides of the quilt, pressing the seams open or toward the borders.

3. Trim 2 of the pieced bg strips to the average width of the quilt top, approximately 46½˝ and sew onto the top and bottom of the quilt, pressing the seams open or toward the borders. The finished quilt top should measure approximately 46½˝ × 46½˝.

alternate colorway

Pieced and quilted by Travis Steward

FABRICS USED

- **Charm pack:** *Pink and black prints from stash*
- **Fabric A:** *Bella Solids in Black by Moda Fabrics*
- **Background:** *Bella Solids in White by Moda Fabrics*

Finishing

For complete instructions, refer to Finishing the Quilt (page 121).

1. Make the quilt backing:

- Remove the selvages. Cut the fabric into 2 pieces (about 55˝ × WOF), and sew the backing pieces together along the trimmed selvage edges, using a ½˝ seam. Press the seam open. Trim to approximately 55˝ × 55˝.

or

- Sew a 16˝ × 55˝ strip onto a 55˝ × WOF piece of fabric to make a 55˝ × 55˝ backing.

2. Layer the quilt top, batting, and backing. Baste and quilt as desired. *Coin Flip* was quilted in a stipple design.

3. Bind and enjoy your quilt!

Charming Stripes

Pieced by Cheryl Brickey and quilted by Carol Alperin

finished quilt

39˝ × 48˝

social media

#CharmingStripesQuilt

Need a quilt that sews up quickly? *Charming Stripes* is one of the fastest quilts to make in the book. The charm squares are the star of this quilt with the fabric A and background fabric framing them.

FABRICS USED

- **Charm pack:** *Reunion by Sweetwater for Moda Fabrics*
- **Fabric A**: *Painter's Palette Solids in Poppy Red by Paintbrush Studios*
- **Background:** *Pure Solids in White Linen by Art Gallery Fabrics*

Fabric Requirements

Width of fabric (WOF) is assumed to be at least 40˝.

CHARM SQUARES (5˝ × 5˝): 34

FABRIC A (RED): ⅝ yard

BACKGROUND (BG) (CREAM): 1 yard

BINDING (STRAIGHT GRAIN): ½ yard

BACKING: 2⅝ yards *or* 1⅝ yards with a 8˝ × 56˝ strip pieced on

BATTING: 47˝ × 56˝˝

Cutting

CHARM SQUARES

- Cut 12 charm squares in half to make 24 rectangles 2½˝ × 5˝.
- Trim 2 charm squares to 3¾˝ × 5˝.
- The remaining 20 charm squares will be used as 5˝ × 5˝ squares.

FABRIC A (RED)

- Cut 9 strips 2˝ × WOF for sashing columns.

BACKGROUND (BG) (CREAM)

- Cut 3 strips 5½˝ × WOF for background columns.
- Cut 3 strips 3½˝ × WOF for background columns.

BINDING

- Cut 5 strips 2½˝ × WOF.

Piecing and Preparing the Columns

Use a scant ¼˝ (a thread width smaller than ¼˝) seam throughout the construction of the quilt top unless otherwise instructed.

Column A

1. Sew together the following pieces in an alternating arrangement, pressing the seams open or toward the charm fabric rectangles to make a column 5˝ × 48˝.

- 7 charm squares 5˝ × 5˝
- 8 charm fabric rectangles 2½˝ × 5˝

2. Repeat Step 1 to make a total of 2 column A.

Column B

Sew together the following pieces as shown, starting and ending with the charm fabric rectangles 3¾˝ × 5˝, pressing the seams open or toward the charm fabric rectangles to make 1 column B 5˝ × 48˝.

- 6 charm squares 5˝ × 5˝
- 2 charm fabric rectangles 3¾˝ × 5˝
- 7 charm fabric rectangles 2½˝ × 5˝

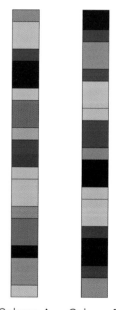

Column A   Column B

Sashing Columns

1. Cut 3 fabric A strips 2″ × WOF in half to make 6 half-fabric A strips 2″ × about 20″.

2. Sew each half-fabric A strip to a full fabric A strip 2″ × WOF and trim to 48″ to make 6 sashing columns 2″ × 48″.

Background Columns

1. Cut a bg fabric strip 3½″ × WOF in half, sew each half-bg strip to a full bg strip 3½″ × WOF, and trim to 48″ to make 2 inner bg columns 3½″ × 48″.

2. Cut a bg fabric strip 5½″ × WOF in half, sew each half-bg strip to a full bg strip 5½″ × WOF, and trim to 48″ to make 2 outer bg columns 5½″ × 48″.

Quilt Top Assembly

Arrange and sew together the columns listed and as shown, pressing the seams open to make the finished quilt top approximately 39″ × 48″.

- 3 pieced columns 5″ × 48″
- 6 sashing columns 2″ × 48″
- 2 inner bg columns 3½″ × 48″
- 2 outer bg columns 5½″ × 48″

Finishing

For complete instructions, refer to Finishing the Quilt (page 121).

1. Make the quilt backing:

- Remove the selvages. Cut the fabric into 2 pieces (about 47″ × WOF), and sew the backing pieces together along the trimmed selvage edges, using a ½″ seam. Press the seam open. Trim to approximately 46″ × 57″.

or

- Sew a 8″ × 56″ strip onto a 56″ × WOF piece of fabric to make a 47″ × 56″ backing.

2. Layer the quilt top, batting, and backing. Baste and quilt as desired. *Charming Stripes* was quilted in a floral design.

3. Bind and enjoy your quilt!

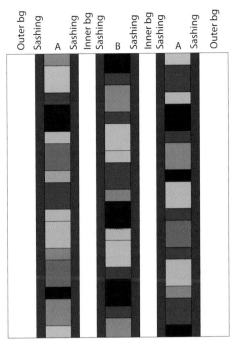

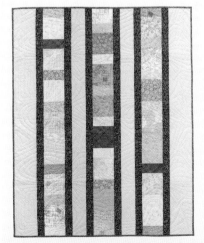

alternate colorway

Pieced by Cheryl Brickey and quilted by Carol Alperin

FABRICS USED

- **Charm pack:** *Various Carolyn Friedlander prints for Robert Kaufman Fabrics*
- **Fabric A:** *Letter in Black from the Architextures collection by Carolyn Friedlander for Robert Kaufman Fabrics*
- **Background:** *Crosshatch in Gray from the Architextures collection by Carolyn Friedlander for Robert Kaufman Fabrics*

Blossom Chains

Pieced by Cheryl Brickey and quilted by Carol Alperin

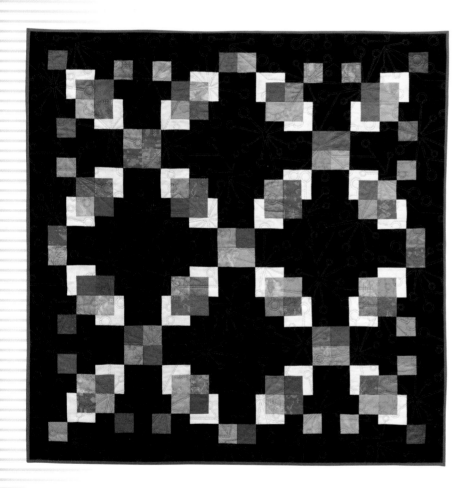

finished block

10″ × 10″

finished quilt

44½″ × 44½″

social media

#BlossomChainsQuilt

Blossom Chains uses three different, simple block designs that when combined into the quilt top, create a blossomlike effect. My children love the bright rainbow colors of the Sun Print 2020 charm pack, and I felt that a black background would make these colors pop.

FABRICS USED

- **Charm pack:** *Sun Print 2020 by Alison Glass for Andover Fabrics*

- **Fabric A**: *Bella Solids in White by Moda Fabrics*

- **Background:** *Bella Solids in Black by Moda Fabrics*

Fabric Requirements

Width of fabric (WOF) is assumed to be at least 40˝.

CHARM SQUARES (5˝ × 5˝): 28

FABRIC A (WHITE): ⅓ yard

BACKGROUND (BG) (BLACK): 1⅝ yards

BINDING (STRAIGHT GRAIN): ½ yard

BACKING: 3 yards or 1½ yards with a 14˝ × 53˝ strip pieced on

BATTING: 53˝ × 53˝

Cutting

CHARM SQUARES

- Cut 20 charm squares in half horizontally and vertically to make 80 charm fabric squares 2½˝ × 2½˝.

- The remaining 8 charm squares will be used as 5˝ × 5˝ squares.

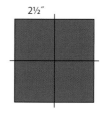
2½˝

FABRIC A (WHITE)

- Cut 6 strips 1½˝ × WOF.

  Subcut 4 strips into 16 rectangles 1½˝ × 7˝ (each strip can yield 5 rectangles).

  Subcut 2 strips into 16 rectangles 1½˝ × 5˝ (each strip can yield 8 rectangles).

BACKGROUND (BG) (BLACK)

- Cut 8 strips 3½˝ × WOF.

  Subcut 3 strips into 16 rectangles 3½˝ × 5½˝ (each strip can yield 7 rectangles).

  Subcut 5 strips into 80 rectangles 3½˝ × 2½˝ (each strip can yield 16 rectangles).

- Cut 7 strips 2½˝ × WOF.

  Subcut 2 strips into 32 squares 2½˝ × 2½˝ (each strip can yield 16 squares).
  Reserve 5 strips for border.

- Cut 5 strips 1½˝ × WOF.

  Subcut 3 strips into 16 rectangles 1½˝ × 5½˝ (each strip can yield 7 rectangles).

  Subcut 2 strips into 16 rectangles 1½˝ × 4½˝ (each strip can yield 8 rectangles).

BINDING

- Cut 5 strips 2½˝ × WOF.

Piecing the Units and Blocks

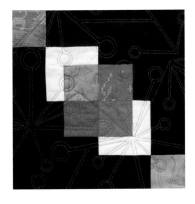

Use a scant ¼˝ (a thread width smaller than ¼˝) seam throughout the construction of the quilt top unless otherwise instructed.

X Units

1. Sew the fabric A rectangles 1½˝ × 5˝ on either side of a charm square 5˝ × 5˝.

2. Sew the fabric rectangles 1½˝ × 7˝ on the top and bottom, pressing the seams open or toward the charm square to make a unit 7˝ × 7˝.

3. Repeat Steps 1 and 2 to make a total of 8 units 7˝ × 7˝.

4. Cut each unit from Step 3 in half vertically and horizontally into 4 quarters 3½˝ × 3½˝ (the cut line will be 3½˝ from the edge) to make a total of 32 quarters.

5. Sew together the following units and pieces as shown, pressing the seams open, to make an X unit 5½˝ × 5½˝.

- 1 quarter 3½˝ × 3½˝
- 2 bg rectangles 2½˝ × 3½˝
- 1 charm fabric square 2½˝ × 2½˝

6. Repeat Step 5 to make a total of 32 X units.

Y Units

1. Sew together the following pieces, pressing the seams open, to make a Y unit 5½˝ × 5½˝.

- 1 charm fabric square 2½˝ × 2½˝
- 1 bg rectangle 3½˝ × 5½˝
- 1 bg rectangle 2½˝ × 3½˝

2. Repeat Step 1 to make a total of 16 Y units.

Z Units

1. Sew together the following pieces, pressing the seams open or toward the bg squares, to make a four-patch unit 4½˝ × 4½˝.

- 2 charm fabric squares 2½˝ × 2½˝
- 2 bg squares 2½˝ × 2½˝

2. Sew a bg rectangle 1½˝ × 4½˝ on one side of a four-patch unit 4½˝ × 4½˝ from Step 1, pressing the seam open.

3. Sew a bg rectangle 1½˝ × 5½˝ on the bottom of the unit from Step 2, pressing the seam open, to make a Z unit 5½˝ × 5½˝.

4. Repeat Steps 1–3 to make a total of 16 Z units 5½˝ × 5½˝.

A Blocks

1. Sew together the following units, pressing the seams open, to make an A block 10½˝ × 10½˝ (10˝ × 10˝ in the finished quilt top).

- 2 X units 5½˝ × 5½˝
- 2 Y units 5½˝ × 5½˝

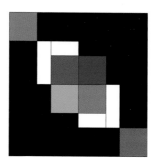

2. Repeat Step 1 to make a total of 4 A blocks.

B Blocks

1. Sew together the following units, pressing the seams open, to make a B block 10½˝ × 10½˝ (10˝ × 10˝ in the finished quilt top).

- 2 X units 5½˝ × 5½˝
- 1 Y unit 5½˝ × 5½˝
- 1 Z unit 5½˝ × 5½˝

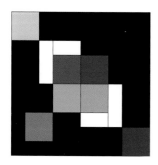

2. Repeat Step 1 to make a total of 8 B blocks.

C Blocks

1. Sew together the following blocks, pressing the seams open, to make an A block 10½˝ × 10½˝ (10˝ × 10˝ in the finished quilt top).

- 2 X units 5½˝ × 5½˝
- 2 Z units 5½˝ × 5½˝

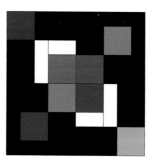

2. Repeat Step 1 to make a total of 4 C blocks.

Quilt Top Assembly

1. Arrange the following blocks in a 4 × 4 arrangement (4 rows of 4 blocks each), making sure that the orientation of the blocks matches the quilt top assembly diagram.

- 4 block A 10½″ × 10½″
- 8 block B 10½″ × 10½″
- 4 block C 10½″ × 10½″

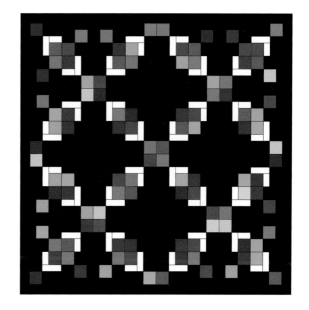

C	B	B	C
A	A
B	A	A	B
B	A	A	B
C	B	B	C

2. Sew the blocks into rows and sew the rows together, pressing the seams open. The quilt top, before the borders are added, should measure 40½″ × 40½″.

Border

tip BORDER LENGTH

Some fabrics have a width of fabric (WOF) wider than the 40″ assumed by this pattern. If your fabric has a WOF of at least 40½″, then you do not need to piece your fabric for the side borders (Step 2, below).

1. Cut 1 bg strip 2½″ × WOF into 4 pieces (2½″ × about 10″) and sew each bg piece 2½″ × about 10″ to a full bg strip 2½″ × WOF.

2. Trim 2 of the pieced bg strips to the average height of the quilt top, approximately 40½″, and sew onto the sides of the quilt, pressing the seams open or toward the borders.

3. Trim 2 of the pieced bg strips to the average width of the quilt top, approximately 44½″, and sew onto the top and bottom of the quilt, pressing the seams open or toward the borders. The finished quilt top should measure 44½″ × 44½″.

Finishing

For complete instructions, refer to Finishing the Quilt (page 121).

1. Make the quilt backing:

- Remove the selvages. Cut the fabric into 2 pieces (about 53″ × WOF), and sew the backing pieces together along the trimmed selvage edges, using a ½″ seam. Press the seam open. Trim to approximately 53″ × 53″.

or

- Sew a 14″ × 53″ strip onto a 53″ × WOF piece of fabric to make a 53″ × 53″ backing.

2. Layer the quilt top, batting, and backing. Baste and quilt as desired. *Blossom Chains* was quilted in a star burst–like design.

3. Bind and enjoy your quilt!

alternate colorway

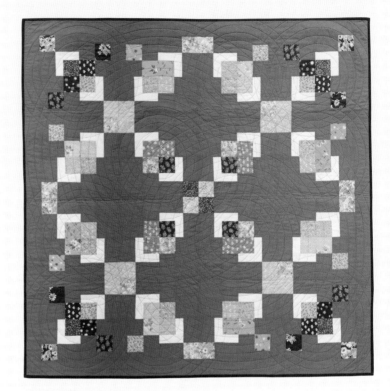

Pieced and quilted by Yvonne Fuchs

FABRICS USED

- **Charm pack:** *Flour Garden by Linzee Kull McCray for Moda Fabrics*
- **Fabric A:** *Bella Solids in White by Moda Fabrics*
- **Background:** *Shot Cotton in Pool by Kaffe Fassett for FreeSpirit Fabrics*

For all the quilts featured in this book, the charm squares can be placed randomly (typically attempting to get an even distribution of colors and prints across the quilt top). Another option is to do what Yvonne did and place the charm squares strategically so that the colors of the charm squares are in set locations in the quilt top. This provides a different and interesting look to the quilt.

Goose in the Pond

Pieced and quilted
by Cheryl Brickey

finished block

18¾″ × 18¾″

finished quilt

44″ × 48″

social media

#GooseinthePondQuilt

Goose in the Pond is a fun take on the classic Goose in the Pond quilt block. With only four blocks and simple strip piecing, the quilt comes together quickly and easily.

Fabric Requirements

Width of fabric (WOF) is assumed to be at least 40˝.

CHARM SQUARES (5˝ × 5˝): 28

FABRIC A (WHITE): 1¼ yards

BACKGROUND (BG) (TEAL): 1¼ yards

BINDING (STRAIGHT GRAIN): ½ yard

BACKING: 2⅞ yards
or 1⅝ yards with a 13˝ × 56˝ strip pieced on

BATTING: 52˝ × 56˝

Cutting

CHARM SQUARES

- Trim 4 charm squares to 4¼˝ × 4¼˝.

- The remaining 24 charm squares will be used as 5˝ × 5˝ squares.

FABRIC A (WHITE)

- Cut 3 strips 5˝ × WOF.

  Subcut the strips into 24 squares 5˝ × 5˝ (each strip can yield 8 squares).

- Cut 2 strips 4¼˝ × WOF.

  Subcut the strips into 16 squares 4¼˝ × 4¼˝ (each strip can yield 9 squares).

- Cut 7 strips 1¾˝ × WOF.

BACKGROUND (BG) (TEAL)

- Cut 3 strips 4½˝ × WOF for borders.

- Cut 4 strips 2½˝ × WOF.

  Subcut 1 strip into 2 sashing pieces 2½˝ × 19¼˝. Reserve 3 strips for sashing and side borders.

- Cut 8 strips 1¾˝ × WOF.

BINDING

- Cut 5 strips 2½˝ × WOF.

Piecing the Units and Blocks

Use a scant ¼˝ (a thread width smaller than ¼˝) seam throughout the construction of the quilt top unless otherwise instructed.

Striped Units and Checker Units

1. Sew together 2 bg fabric strips 1¾˝ × WOF and 1 fabric A strip 1¾˝ × WOF along their long sides to make an X strip set 4¼˝ × WOF. Press the seams open or toward the darker fabric.

2. Repeat Step 1 to make a total of 3 X strip sets.

FABRICS USED

- **Charm pack:** *Canning Day by Corey Yoder for Moda Fabrics*
- **Fabric A**: *Bella Solids in White by Moda Fabrics*
- **Background:** *Bella Solids in Prussian Blue by Moda Fabrics*

3. Cut 2 X strip sets into 16 striped units 4¼″ × 4¼″ (each first strip set can yield 9 striped units).

4. Cut 1 X strip set into 16 X units 1¾″ × 4¼″.

5. Sew together 2 fabric A strips 1¾″ × WOF and 1 bg fabric strip 1¾″ × WOF along their long sides to make a Y strip set 4¼″ × WOF. Press the seams open or toward the darker fabric.

6. Repeat Step 5 to make a total of 2 Y strip sets.

7. Cut the Y strip sets into 32 Y units 1¾″ × 4¼″ (each second strip set can yield 22 Y units).

8. Sew together 1 X unit 1¾″ × 4¼″ and 2 Y units 1¾″ × 4¼″, pressing the seams open to make a checker unit 4¼″ × 4¼″.

9. Repeat Step 8 to make a total of 16 checker units.

Half-Square Triangle (HST) Units

1. Place a charm square 5″ × 5″ and a fabric A square 5″ × 5″ right sides together. Draw a diagonal line using a removable marking device on the back of the lighter square (shown as the solid line).

2. Sew a ¼″ seam on both sides of the solid line (shown as the dotted lines). Cut on the solid line and press the seam open or toward the darker fabric.

3. Trim the HST unit to 4¼″ × 4¼″. *Each set of 1 charm square and 1 fabric A square will yield 2 HST units.*

4. Repeat Steps 1–3 to make a total of 48 HST units 4¼″ × 4¼″.

tip **HST UNIT SIZE**

Note that the HST units are trimmed to 4¼″ × 4¼″ instead of the typical 4½″ × 4½″.

Block Assembly

1. Arrange the following pieces, making sure that the orientation of the pieces matches the illustration.

- 12 HST units 4¼″ × 4¼″
- 1 charm fabric square 4¼″ × 4¼″
- 4 checker units 4¼″ × 4¼″
- 4 striped units 4¼″ × 4¼″
- 4 fabric A squares 4¼″ × 4¼″

2. Sew the pieces into rows, pressing the seams open or as indicated by the arrows.

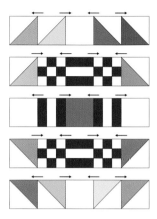

3. Sew the rows together, pressing the seams open, to make a block 19¼″ × 19¼″ (18¾″ × 18¾″ in the finished quilt top).

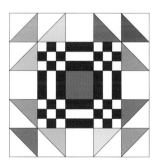

4. Repeat Step 3 to make a total of 4 blocks

Quilt Top Assembly

1. Sew together 2 blocks 19¼″ × 19¼″ and 1 bg sashing piece 2½″ × 19¼″, pressing the seams open or toward the sashing, to make a block row 19¼″ × 40″.

2. Repeat Step 1 to make 2 block rows.

3. Trim 1 bg strip 2½″ × WOF to 40″ to make a sashing row. Sew together the 2 block rows and the sashing row. The quilt top, before borders are added, should measure 40″ × 40″.

Border

1. Trim 2 bg strips 2½″ × WOF to the average height of the quilt, approximately 40″. Sew the side borders onto the quilt top, pressing the seams open or toward the borders.

2. Cut 1 bg strip 4½″ × WOF in half and sew each half to a full bg strip 4½″ × WOF. Trim to the average width of the quilt, approximately 44″. Sew the borders onto the top and bottom of the quilt top, pressing the seams open or toward the borders. The quilt top should measure approximately 44″ × 48″.

Finishing

For complete instructions, refer to Finishing the Quilt (page 121).

1. Make the quilt backing:

- Remove the selvages. Cut the fabric into 2 pieces (about 52″ × WOF), and sew the backing pieces together along the trimmed selvage edges, using a ½″ seam. Press the seam open. Trim to approximately 52″ × 56″.

  or

- Sew a 13″ × 56″ strip onto a 56″ × WOF piece of fabric to make a 52″ × 56″ backing.

2. Layer the quilt top, batting, and backing. Baste and quilt as desired. *Goose in the Pond* was quilted in a large paisley design.

3. Bind and enjoy your quilt!

alternate colorway

Pieced and quilted by Darleen Sanford

FABRICS USED

- **Charm pack:** *Amethyst Garden by Melissa Lowry for Clothworks*
- **Fabric A:** *Bella Solids in White by Moda Fabrics*
- **Background:** *Bella Solids in Charcoal by Moda Fabrics*

Finishing the Quilt

Make the Quilt Sandwich

1. Lay the backing wrong side up and tape the edges down with masking tape. If you are working on carpet you can use T-pins to secure the backing to the carpet.

2. Center the batting on top of the backing, smoothing out any folds and creases.

3. Center the quilt top, right side up, on top of the batting.

Basting

Basting keeps the quilt sandwich layers from shifting while quilting.

Basting options:

- Use a temporary spray adhesive between the backing/batting and the batting/quilt top. Follow the manufacturer's directions, use in a well-ventilated area, and protect the surrounding area from overspray.
- Pin the quilt layers together with safety pins placed about 3″–4″ apart. Begin basting in the center and move toward the edges.
- Baste by hand with thread.
- Ask a longarm quilter to baste the quilt.

Quilting

Quilting, whether by machine or hand, serves to attach all three layers of the quilt sandwich together and can enhance the design of the quilt. The 36 quilts in this book showcase many different quilting designs from walking foot quilting to free motion quilting to professional longarm quilting.

Binding the Quilt

Trim excess batting and backing from the quilt even with the edges of the quilt top squaring up if necessary.

Make the Binding

1. Cut the binding strips crosswise (from selvage to selvage) and piece them together with diagonal seams, as shown, to make a continuous binding strip. Trim the seam allowances to ¼″.

Sew.

Trim.

2. Press the seams open.

3. Press the entire strip in half lengthwise with wrong sides together.

Attach the Binding

1. Pin the binding to the edge of the front of the quilt top (raw edges of the binding and quilt top aligned) along one side of the quilt and leave the first 8″–10″ inches of the binding unattached.

2. Sew the binding onto the quilt top with ¼″ seam allowance.

3. Stop ¼″ away from the first corner, back stitch, and cut the thread. Rotate the quilt one-quarter turn.

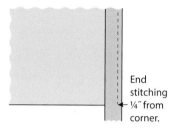

End stitching ¼″ from corner.

4. Fold the binding at a right angle so it extends straight above the quilt and the fold forms a 45° angle in the corner.

First fold

5. Bring the binding strip down even with the edge of the quilt and begin sewing the next side of the quilt from the folded edge. Repeat for all the corners.

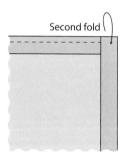

Second fold

6. Continue stitching until 10″–12″ from where the binding was first sewn to the quilt. Overlap the binding ends at a point near the middle of the gap between the starting and stopping points.

Cut the binding tails so that they lap over 2½″ (the width of the binding strip).

7. Open both binding ends and place one end on top of the other end at right angles, right sides together. Mark a diagonal line from corner to corner and stitch on the line. Check that the binding fits the quilt; then trim the seam allowance to ¼″. Finger press the seam open.

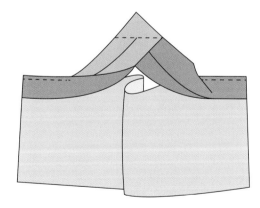

8. Stitch this last binding section in place on the quilt.

9. Fold the binding over to the quilt back and hand stitch in place mitering the corners, or if you prefer machine stitch the binding to the back of the quilt.

Pattern Coloring Pages

These pages can be used to test out color schemes and quilting designs for the quilts. The pages are also available online as PDFs that you may download and print:

tinyurl.com/11440-patterns-download

Windows Coloring Diagram

(For project, see page 16.)

Medallion Coloring Diagram

(For project, see page 23.)

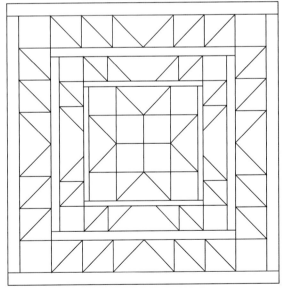

Fishies Coloring Diagram

(For project, see page 30.)

Star Surround Coloring Diagram

(For project, see page 38.)

Ships Ahoy Coloring Diagram

(For project, see page 44.)

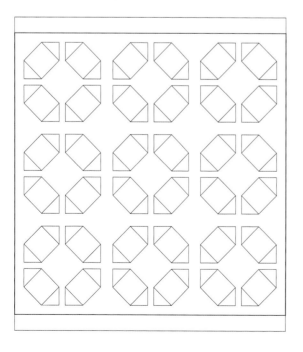

Cat's Eye Coloring Diagram

(For project, see page 50.)

Magic Carpet Coloring Diagram

(For project, see page 54.)

Circus Stars Coloring Diagram

(For project, see page 61.)

Cozy Cottages Coloring Diagram

(For project, see page 67.)

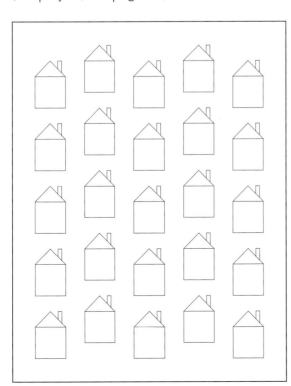

Ninja Coloring Diagram

(For project, see page 73.)

Bowtie Coloring Diagram

(For project, see page 79.)

Nine-Patch Challenge Coloring Diagram

(For project, see page 84.)

One-Eyed Monster Coloring Diagram

(For project, see page 89.)

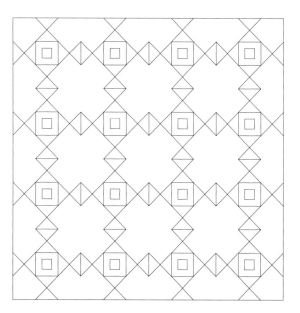

Baskets Coloring Diagram

(For project, see page 94.)

Coin Flip Coloring Diagram

(For project, see page 100.)

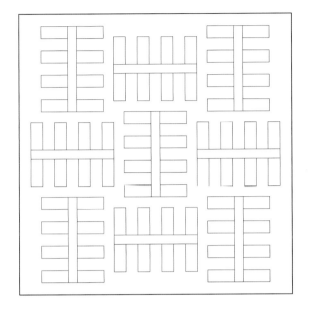

Charming Stripes Coloring Diagram

(For project, see page 104.)

Blossom Chains Coloring Diagram

(For project, see page 108.)

Goose in the Pond Coloring Diagram

(For project, see page 115.)

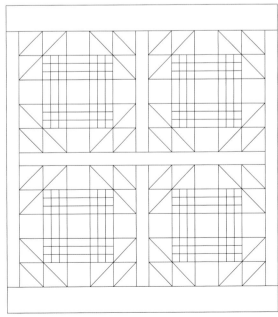

About the Author

Cheryl Brickey began quilting in 2010 to make her daughter (then a toddler) a quilt for her first bed, and she has been quilting nonstop since. She was born and raised in New Jersey and now calls South Carolina home, where she and her husband are

Photo by Melissa Dorn

raising their two children. Cheryl has a chemical engineering degree from Carnegie Mellon University and spends her days writing patent applications for a private textile and chemical company. She combines her technical writing, engineering, and math skills in each of her quilt designs, with quilt math being one of her favorite elements to pattern writing.

Cheryl is an active member of the Greenville Modern Quilt Guild and is also very involved with the online quilting community. She has taught modern quilt design, sewing and quilting techniques, and computer-aided quilt design across the country to guilds and at national quilt shows.

Cheryl has won numerous awards for her quilts and designs. She has been featured on the *Moda Bake Shop* blog; in *Modern Quilts Unlimited*, *Quiltmaker*, *Modern Patchwork*, *Make Modern*, and *Quilty* magazines; and in QuiltCon and other international quilt shows.

Cheryl's first book, *Modern Plus Sign Quilts*, coauthored with Paige Alexander, explored her love of the traditional plus sign block.

Visit Cheryl online and follow on social media!

Website:
meadow-mist-designs.com

Blog:
meadowmistdesigns.blogspot.com

Instagram:
@meadowmistdesigns

Pinterest:
/meadowmistdesigns

Facebook:
/meadowmistdesigns

About the Quilter

Carol Alperin longarm quilted almost half the quilts in this book. Her quilting obsession started in 1998 when her daughter left for college. After quilting many quilts including three queen-size quilts on my domestic machine, she bought an Innova longarm in 2009. Carol's quilting passion has shifted from piecing to machine quilting as she grew her Upstairs Quilting business. She has been blessed with a supportive husband and priceless quilting friends. You can find Carol at home quilting upstairs in Summerville, South Carolina, or on Instagram at @carolaquilter.

By Cheryl Brickey and Paige Alexander: